Out of the
Black Hole

Out of the
Black Hole

The Patient's Guide
to Vagus Nerve Stimulation
and Depression

CHARLES E. DONOVAN, III

Wellness Publishers, LLC

First Edition

Copyright © 2005 Charles E. Donovan, III

Published by Wellness Publishers, LLC
www.VagusNerveStimulator.com

Library of Congress Control Number: 2004114168

Donovan, Charles E.
Out of the black hole : the patient's guide to vagus nerve stimulation and depression / Charles E. Donovan. — St. Louis, MO : Wellness Publishers, 2005.

  p. ; cm.
  ISBN 0-9748484-1-7

  1. Donovan, Charles E.—Health. 2. Depressed persons—Care.
3. Depression, Mental—Treatment. 4. Neural stimulation. I. Title.

RC537 .D66 2005
616.85/27—dc22   0411

Cover & Text Design: Mary Jo Zazueta / www.tothepointsolutions.com

To my family, who never gave up hope,
even when I had lost all hope.

Contents

FOREWORD

The devastating effects of long-term, chronic depression can barely be imagined by those who are exempt from its grip and can barely be described by those who suffer in its shadow. In the thirty years of my practice in psychology and social work, too many times I have watched lives being consumed by the illness. The added layer of shame for suffering from an illness that is not seen as quite "legitimate" by friends and relatives, makes it even more difficult. Isolation is often the only alternative when it feels so hard to be with others and feel so alone. Worse yet, those who love someone who is depressed, often say "just buck up" and "you can get over it" in an effort to cheer them up.

It has been a joy to watch the transformation of Mr. Donovan as he has emerged from his depression of many years. When I met him, he was completely isolated and woke every day emotionally paralyzed by his illness. Now he has moved from his extreme self-focus to seeing friends and family, and finally to writing this book as a way to help others. He has achieved a sense of perspective about his life that is demonstrated by his dry sense of humor.

As a therapist, I often learn as much from my patients as I hope they learn from me. Working with Mr. Donovan has been one of

those experiences. I believe I have never met anyone more committed to his recovery. He was willing to do anything to feel better,
including becoming a participant in the vagus nerve study. In this
book, he describes the descent into his illness with humor and
pathos. Then he goes on to describe the surgery that led to his
recovery. His willingness to rise above his own shame about his suffering so that others can learn about a new and exciting treatment
is admirable. This book is a must read for anyone, whether layper-
son or professional, who is seeking hope for the treatment of
depression.

NANCY WILLIGER, PhD

ACKNOWLEDGMENTS

The author gratefully acknowledges the following individuals and organizations:

Richard Bucholz, MD; Charles Conway, MD; Marc Deschamps; Eduardo Garcia-Ferrer, MD; JoAnn Filla-Taylor, RN; Linda Greensfelder, PhD; Rachel Feinberg, MD; Hara Estroff Murano; Roxann Schroeder, PhD; Amy Schoenfeld; Raymond Tait, PhD; Amanda Tennant, MSPT; Tony Vitale, LMT; Nancy Williger, PhD; Mary Jo Zazueta; Patient Advocate Foundation; *Psychology Today Magazine*; and St. Louis University Hospital.

And a special thank you to each and every one of the 500 employees at Cyberonics, who tirelessly researched and developed this extraordinary life-saving, life-altering medical device.

Introduction

Everybody has a story. My story is the one I know best and can write about. It is not a memoir of chemical dependency or self-abuse. Those subjects have been written about many times. This is a story of my winning battle against depression and the vagus nerve stimulation treatment that saved my life by bringing me *Out of the Black Hole*. And, this is the first book to be published about winning the battle with a medical implant procedure called VNS Therapy™.

Personally, I don't believe the stigma associated with depression has changed one bit in the past century, so I was apprehensive about sharing my story. After all, I had spent the majority of my life *hiding* my depression from family, friends, and business associates--and now I was writing a tell-all book.

I wrote the main part of this book as if I were having a conversation with my closest friend who was looking for guidance with his or her debilitating chronic depression. I discuss the misery I experienced, the seemingly unending search for answers, the vagus nerve implant procedure itself, and my subsequent recovery from the grip of depression.

The last part, the appendices, contains technical information about depression; the VNS Therapy System™; and Cyberonics, the manufacturer of the vagus nerve stimulator.

I hope my journey and the treatment I chose helps readers with their depression treatment plans; especially when they consider whether or not to undergo vagus nerve stimulation therapy. When I decided to participate in the investigational trial there wasn't any information available to me. I just signed an eleven-page consent agreement and hoped for the best.

On June 15, 2004, the FDA's Medical Device Advisory Panel recommended approval of vagus nerve stimulation as an adjunctive long-term treatment for chronic depression. Cyberonics, the manufacturer of the VNS Therapy System™, is in the process of providing the FDA additional information required for the FDA to render a final decision consistent with the Panel's recommendation. Currently VNS Therapy for the treatment of chronic depression is available in Canada and Europe.

I also wrote *Out of the Black Hole: The Patient's Guide to Vagus Nerve Stimulation and Depression* for the loved ones of people who suffer from depression. When a patient reaches the severe, chronic level of this disease, often it is their family members who are making the medical decisions. At the other extreme, the family members may be in the dark about what is going on between the doctor and the patient, or they don't trust the information that they're receiving from their loved ones. One thing is for certain, the lack of knowledge about this disease and not knowing the best way to help and interact with the suffering loved one complicates everything.

I have been fortunate throughout my life because I have always had access to the best medical care available (for any illness), and I have a close and supportive family. I don't know how people survive severe depression if they don't have access to good doctors, the latest pharmaceutical drugs, psychologists, psychiatrists, and a strong support group. Many depressed patients have none of the above, yet they still endure. Their stories, in many ways, are more remarkable than mine.

Senator Hillary Rodham Clinton wrote a book titled *It Takes a Village*. It's about how we can shape our society into the kind of village that enables children to grow into able, caring, resilient adults; physically, intellectually, emotionally, and spiritually. If my family wrote a similar book about the past ten years of my life, it would be titled *It Took Heaven and Earth*. So, I've also written this book for them. Let's get started.

chapter one

THE STIGMA OF DEPRESSION

Have you ever watched a television show where a famous celebrity dispenses the advice: "Just take your antidepressants and you'll get better?" I have, and it really makes me mad. For instance, one night I was watching the *Larry King Show* on CNN and Mike Wallace was the guest. Mr. Wallace has courageously and bravely talked publicly about his long struggle with depression. I applaud him for that. It took a lot of guts.

On this particular night, at the end of the show, Mr. Wallace pointed to the camera and said, "Take the antidepressants prescribed by your doctor, because they work." But he left out two critical words: "for him." They work for him. And he is damn lucky that the antidepressants work. It's pure luck of the draw whether or not antidepressants work for a depressed person. It's not a character flaw or due to a person's laziness; it's simply that the chemical balances oftentimes don't work.

Imagine walking through the borough of Manhattan, population 1.2 million people. It's crowded. The number of people nationwide who are not helped by antidepressants is FOUR times greater. At least 4.8 million Americans suffer from chronic or treatment-resistant depression. None of the available antidepressants work for them. I doubt that Mr. Wallace has to check with the human resource's department at CBS to see how many mental health office visits he is allowed each year or what his co-payments are for a brand-name antidepressant. (I am not picking on Mr. Wallace; he is a skilled reporter and an early supporter of mental health issues. I admire him for being the first major celebrity to bring his depression out of the closet and share it with the public.)

Chronic depression is a biological illness, just like cardiovascular disease and cancer. Depression is not in your head; it is in your brain. Depression is now recognized as a neurodegenerative disorder. Prolonged depression may result in progressive and cumulative damage to the brain. *Psychology Today Magazine* summarized the latest findings about depression, as presented at the American Psychiatric Association's annual meeting in May 2004 (see Appendix H).

Educate yourself and your family about this disease. You can eliminate a lot of the frustration and confusion about this baffling disease by keeping up-to-date on the latest scientific information.

Many sufferers of depression do not seek help because of the stigma associated with mental illness. Sometimes family and friends contribute to this image when they continually urge a depressed person to "snap out of it" or "get on with your life" or "count your blessings." I know the person means well; but it's time to blow that type of advice out of the water. It doesn't work. In fact, it makes a person feel more ashamed and more depressed.

If things get bad enough, some people become suicidal. Almost 600,000 suicide attempts each year are serious enough to warrant a trip to the emergency room. Suicide is the eighth leading cause of death in the United States, but it is virtually 100 percent preventable with treatment from a mental health caregiver (psychiatrist, psychologist, social worker). Unfortunately, there is a successful suicide attempt every hour, twenty-four hours a day, seven days a week. Although women are more predisposed to depression than men, four times more men actually commit suicide. Personally, I think the suicide statistics and the number of people suffering from chronic depression are under-reported.

chapter two

INTO THE BLACK HOLE

Although this chapter is at the beginning of the book, it was one of the last chapters I actually wrote. Much to the chagrin of my editor, the thought of writing about my personal experience with depression was the greatest source of procrastination for me. I dreaded it. I didn't know what to say. It felt too invasive.

For insight on how to get started, I read the memoirs of people who suffered from depression. It only made things harder. While I found many self-help books on the subject of depression, I couldn't find any firsthand stories of lengthy battles with chronic depression. There were many different stories, but none that I could relate to.

There were stories written by people with manic and bipolar depression. Some of these people would book a first-class airline ticket to France on a moment's notice, gamble a hundred thousand dollars in Monte Carlo, have sex with all sorts of creatures, drop fifty thousand dollars on a shopping spree in Paris, return to the States, and then crash after having been awake for seventy-two hours straight. I couldn't believe what I was reading. It was incredible, but it wasn't me.

There were a few books even more dramatic and serious, about people with histories of multiple suicide attempts, paranoid schizophrenia, and numerous personality disorders. Once again, these weren't in any way related to my experience with depression.

I worried that readers would be bored to death by the simplicity of my life, a garden-variety patient suffering from severe chronic depression. Or even worse, I feared my depression was some sort of bizarre or abnormal illness. It's one thing to have depression, but it's another thing to have had weird depression. I needed a catalyst to get this chapter going. So, recently, during the last two minutes of an appointment with my psychologist, I sheepishly squeezed in a quick question: "I just want to make sure that what I told you about the way I felt and what I did, do you hear that type of stuff from other patients?"

She nodded and said, "Yes, I hear the same exact information from many of my patients suffering from depression."

I was relieved. I'm normal—whatever that means. Having been inspired by the doctor's answer, I decided it was time to finally start this chapter and get it over with. However, the main purpose of this book is to educate people about vagus nerve stimulation therapy for depression. It's not going to be a long, detailed journey about my battle with depression. That's far too dull. But I think some of this information is necessary to clarify why I qualified for inclusion in the investigational study.

I am going to speed through the first forty years of my life. They are important, but the past five years are much more significant to this book.

There is a history of depression on both sides of my family. As in most families, it wasn't talked about. Within my immediate family, I got the gene. On December 9, 1968, when I was eleven, my mother tragically died in a house fire.

In 1968, medical wisdom said children didn't get depressed. Ironically, I kept hearing this over and over: "Children are resilient, they bounce back quickly." The reality, however, was that I was completely devastated by my mother's death. I never got the chance to say good-bye. I never had the chance to tell her how much I loved her one last time. I am still haunted by that night.

Today we know children do get depressed; I guess I was just ahead of my time. We also know that most depressive episodes are preceded by a stressful event. I have never discussed this with my father, but in the summer of 1969 I was sent off to camp. My other three siblings (all younger) were not. I can only assume I was not bouncing back quickly.

In another strange twist, my roommate at the camp committed suicide in 2002. I had known him for thirty-three years.

My father remarried a year after my mother died and two families were merged together. Three girls and three boys; we were like *The Brady Bunch* gone crazy.

I did not appear to have depression in my teen years. However, in retrospect, it's clear I was suffering from depression. I know I didn't handle stress as well as my siblings did.

It's not that they didn't have their own issues to deal with, but they led normal lives. For me, this was the beginning of isolation, tension, and anxiety. I spent most of my time in my bedroom with the door closed.

I could not understand why I was so stressed out as a child. My brothers and sisters did not feel the same levels of anxiety that I did. Now, I know why: depression. Children, teenagers, and adults with depression do not react the same way to external events as normal people do. Depressed people (including children) have a much more exaggerated reaction to what is going on around them. We take things more personally and seriously.

chapter three

THE 1980s

In the spring of 1980 I was a senior at Georgetown University. After the demise of a close friendship, I had a major depressive episode that lasted for months. I couldn't concentrate, I couldn't pay attention during my classes, and I couldn't study. I feared I would flunk out the second semester of my senior year. Up until that point I had a solid B+ average. But I couldn't do the work anymore. I had little short-term memory. My new motto was "D for diploma."

Finally, out of desperation, I made an appointment with a psychologist at the student health center. I had accepted a job in New York City in the management training program of what is now J.P. Morgan Chase. The only thing I remember about the appointment is that the psychologist told me to get into therapy as soon as I arrived in New York.

In the summer of 1980, I moved to New York. I found a psychologist by going through the yellow pages. In New York, everything is location, location, location. I lived at 141 East 55th

Street, Apt. 5A. I chose a psychologist who had his practice in the same building, Apt. 7N. There was so much shame and stigma of being in psychotherapy that I didn't even tell my roommate I was seeing a psychologist. After my 6:00 p.m. appointment I would walk from the psychologist's office, down two floors to my apartment, and tell my roommate that I was just getting home from work.

That was the beginning of learning how to hide my depression. (It's a skill that people with depression are very good at it.)

After a year with my psychologist "in residence" I switched to a high-profile Park Avenue psychiatrist. He was a published author, had been quoted in *Newsweek* and *Time* magazines, and had been a guest on the *Phil Donahue Show*. At the time, I thought this meant something. It didn't. Of note is that in 1981 a high-profile Park Avenue psychiatrist charged $125 per session compared to $35 per hour for the psychologist in my building. I didn't get my money's worth.

Enough gloom and doom for the moment.

I had a great time in New York in the 1980s. It was an incredibly fun experience. I stayed out late most nights, went to many parties, danced to Lester Lanin and his Orchestra at the Pierre Hotel, dined at Le Cirque, and partied at the Mud Club until closing time. I was a frequent flyer at Studio 54, the Tunnel, the Limelight (before it became tacky), Danceteria, the Palladium, the Surf Club, and Doubles. There were limousine rides to Bruce Springsteen concerts, first-class airline travel, dinner and dancing at The Rainbow Room, countless fourth-row orchestra seats at Broadway shows, a house at the beach every summer, blah, blah, blah.

Living in New York in my twenties was exciting and exhilarating; but it was also a lot of stress on a consistent basis. It never let up.

Stress is not good for people with depression. Fortunately I was able to grind through the stress and depression and have some fun. I was driven to succeed. I read somewhere that you should thrive at your job as opposed to strive. I was striving. There's a subtle difference. It's significantly more work for your mind and body if you are not thriving at work. My depression was manageable and I worked hard not to let things discourage me or get me down. But the depression was always there, lurking in the background.

I drank a lot of alcohol and swallowed many prescription pills. After less than two months in New York (at the age of twenty-one) I did not feel well, so I made an appointment with a medical doctor a few blocks up the street from where I lived (location, location, location). He was a Harvard Medical School graduate in his midseventies. I climbed the steps to his office on the second floor of a walk-up office building. I thought it was a little odd to have an office in a walk-up building. But this was New York City and it was not unusual at all. He gave me a prescription for 2-milligram Valium tablets, which was the lowest available dosage. I had never heard of Valium before, but for me, it turned into "the pause that refreshes." Valium relaxed me. All of a sudden things didn't seem so bad. Valium lowered my anxiety level. I felt better. The "pain" went away. So, I just kept getting the prescription re-filled.

The following year my physician retired, so I went to another doctor, who upped the dosage to 5-milligram tablets. Then I discovered that if I mixed Valium with alcohol I got a better bang for my buck.

Many times I was a nervous wreck at the office. Working on Wall Street is stressful, and if you have depression, you can multiply the stress two- or three-fold. So the doctor upped my dosage to 10-milligram tablets of Valium. My drinking became heavier and my requests for Valium refills were more frequent. Incredibly, I was convinced I had absolutely no drug or alcohol problem.

In 1989 I moved back to my hometown of St. Louis. By then, my drinking had gotten completely out of control, yet still, nobody knew about it. I often drank by myself. Valium was practical because it didn't smell, I could easily carry it with me wherever I went, and, best of all, it had no calories! Many times I took 50 milligrams of Valium throughout the day and then drank three-fourths of a bottle of Wild Turkey or Stoli in the evening and passed out on the couch in my family room. What was I thinking? How could I be so stupid? (And this is a cleaned-up version.)

Thanksgiving 1989. I was in my twentieth day at the Hyland Center, a drug and alcohol treatment facility in St. Louis. Three weeks earlier I told my boss where I was going. He actually thought I was taking a 28-day vacation. Sadly, ignorance about the disease of alcoholism hasn't changed much in fifteen years.

One of my closest friends from seventh grade died of complications from alcoholism in March 2003. I found his body. I didn't know he had a drinking problem until just a few weeks before he died. He was great at hiding and deception and I was really stupid. I, along with his closest friends, had planned an intervention, which ironically was scheduled the day of his funeral. Too little, too late.

Alcoholism and depression often go hand in hand; they now call it "dual diagnosis." I certainly had both. This was back in the heyday of treatment centers. The Hyland Center had a wonderful treatment program. The staff was expertly trained in substance abuse, psychological and mental health problems, and how to help patients recover from their addictions. I was fortunate to have this type of treatment center available to me. I never could have recovered on my own. I was a falling-down drunk and nobody saw it. I know alcoholics are good at hiding and deceiving, but I think people who suffer from depression are even better at hiding their disease, especially since depression doesn't smell like a Wild Turkey Manhattan straight up!

It should be noted that the majority of substance abuse centers have been closed because insurance companies won't pay for residential treatment. Some insurance firms will pay for outpatient treatment, which is mostly worthless. Basically the alcoholic goes to a facility in the morning for a few hours of lectures and then returns home early in the afternoon in time for cocktail hour. It's crazy.

When I first walked into my home on December 4, 1989, after my stay at the Hyland Center, a small artificial Christmas tree was waiting for me on the family room coffee table. A signed card, dated 12-4-89, read: "With Love, Mom and Dad." Christmas 2004 will be the fifteenth time I've used the tree to celebrate my recovery and remind me of my family's continuous love.

My first day back at work (after being away for a month), I was nervous and ashamed. I had a private office less than fifteen feet from the elevators. My plan was to get off the elevator and head straight to my office, unseen. The elevator arrived on the seventh floor and the doors opened. I took three or four steps and then I heard shouting from the other side of the room. "Hey, Charlie's back. Charlie Donovan is back!" Oh brother, my plan hadn't worked.

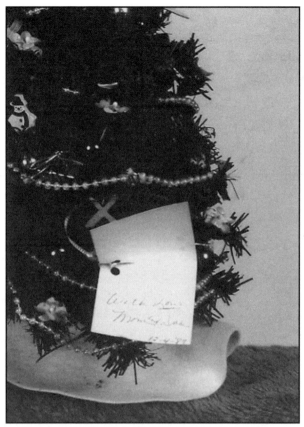

This miniature Christmas tree greeted Charlie on December 4, 1989, upon his return from rehabilitation at the Hyland Center. He still uses the tree each holiday season as a reminder of his sobriety.

O

chapter four

THE 1990S

My depressive episodes gradually became more frequent, severe, and protracted in duration; and it took longer for me to recover from them—until finally I never did recover. This is not an unusual pattern for people suffering from treatment-resistant depression. The depression gets worse and more frequent over the years. I was depressed all the time. Unfortunately, there were no spontaneous expensive trips to Paris, I stayed in one place: the mental health gutter.

In the early 1990s, life was fine. I was completely sober, I earned a good income, and had some fun. But by 1995, I had serious financial setbacks, job turmoil (having nothing to do with my performance), and I was under more stress than I had ever been.

I couldn't eat, couldn't sleep, and woke up every morning at 5:00 a.m., scared to death, with my heart racing in my chest. This anxiety lasted all day, every day. Week after week. Month after month. I would go to work and put on a happy face, but my career was being ruined by the lies and decision making of the senior management of the Wall Street firm I worked for. I foolishly (my fault) kept hoping that management would deliver on their promises to me, but they never did.

Financially, I was taking a beating. The assault on my mind and body from the nonstop stress was brutal. I never got a break, not even for a minute.

In the fall of 1995, the firm that I worked for was named the lead underwriter on a new bond offering. I worked diligently to sell this thing when the offering went public (to large institutional investors). I hustled.

The day came for the deal, November 20, 1995. NAC Re Corporation issued $100,000,000 of 7.15 percent notes due November 15, 2005. I sold more of the offering than any other salesman nationwide, resulting in a net commission to me of $50,000. I was relieved at the end of that long day. But I was not happy.

I must have collapsed or my behavior became alarmingly irrational, because that night my parents hospitalized me. I have no recollection of what happened. I don't even remember being driven to the hospital or being admitted. I had never been a believer in repressed or blocked memories, but I am now.

I remember waking up at 7:30 the next morning. I was lying on a narrow hospital bed, staring at the ceiling, asking myself, "How am I ever going to get my life back?" Then I picked up my cell phone and called my boss. In my cheeriest voice, I said "Hi Richard, it's Charlie."

"Hi Chaz," he said. "You had an unbelievable commission day yesterday; the whole office is talking about it. Great job!"

"Thank you very much," I said. "I appreciate it. But I am feeling a little under the weather today. I won't be coming into the office."

I returned to work about a week later.

I don't know how in the world my cell phone came with me to the hospital. Nine years later, I still don't carry a cell phone on a regular basis. However, that morning it was a good thing I had it with me. Let me gracefully say that I was in a department of the hospital that didn't provide phones with cords in the patients' rooms.

My thinking became more irrational, exaggerated, and unproductive.

We know now that the depressed brain is different than a normal person's brain. The hypothalamus of people with depression tends to be reduced in size, and this can exaggerate normal moods. Consequently, depressed people respond more vigorously to threats from their external environment. Half of all major depressive episodes are preceded by a stress event. This stress event was precipitated by the destruction of my career and financial problems. Things continued to unravel quickly. However, I would never be able to make a rationale, informed decision about my career or find happiness until I could get the albatross of depression off my back. Or more accurately, out of my brain.

From 1994 to 1999, I changed jobs five times. More stress, more anxiety, increased severity of depression. I was searching for happiness and could not find it. In 1998 I accepted a job at a bank with a 90 percent pay cut. I couldn't believe how poorly the employees were treated. I'm not looking for pity, but it was a tough bullet to bite. The shame and stress brought on another major bout of depression.

Although I owned my own home, I had to move back into my

parents' house because I needed their unconditional love and support. I never would have survived without them.

Each morning I'd wake up with my heart pounding and my whole body aching. I'd put on a suit, pump myself up, go to work, and fake contentment all day long. I don't know how I did it. And, eventually, I couldn't do it.

My family had no idea what to do. (No family does.) They were worried, confused, and frustrated. One Saturday morning, as my mom opened the door to the patio for me, she said, "It's a beautiful day. Go take a walk in the park. Just go! Right now!" (If I had a nickel every time someone told me to take a walk in the sunshine because it would make me feel better, I'd be a millionaire.) So, I went for a walk in the park. It was a nice spring day, but I couldn't appreciate the beauty of the blooming dogwood trees or the gorgeous color of the budding azaleas. I couldn't smell the fresh sweetness of the spring air. I was unable to experience any joy or pleasure. I only felt pain, misery, and emptiness. The dichotomy between the beautiful day and how I felt on the inside only made me feel worse.

About fifteen minutes later, my mom drove to the park to find me. "Get in the car," she said. "Your psychiatrist wants to see you. Now!" Apparently as soon as I'd left for the park, Mom placed a desperate call to his office. She pleaded with him and said there must be something more that he could do to help her son. She couldn't believe there was *nothing* left to try. Realize at this point, I had been on every possible combination of antidepressants and antipsychotic medications available. And I was still religiously taking all the medications that he had prescribed, but they were not working.

My parents drove me to the psychiatrist's office. They were full of hope but I had low expectations. My psychiatrist had run out of bullets, and I knew it. I didn't know what more he could say, but at least he could validate that I had tried all the available medications. People lose credibility when they have depression, so I was glad my parents would hear the information directly from the psychiatrist. I know sometimes they didn't believe I was doing all that I could.

This is a partial list of the medications that had been prescribed for me over the years. None of them gave me long-term relief. They are in no particular order.

Imipramine	Lithium	Remeron
Prozac	Effexor	Provigil
Serzone	Wellbutrin	Trazodone
Nortriptyline	Zyprexa	Risperdal
Zoloft	Elavil	Paxil

A nurse ushered us into the doctor's office. We talked for about ten minutes, and then he said, "Well, there is one more thing we could try." My parents and I moved to the edge of our seats. What was it? Then he dropped a bombshell: shock treatments. There was a minute of silence before he explained the procedure carefully and thoroughly. I said okay to a series of electroconvulsive treatments (ECT). There was no negotiation necessary. I was willing to try anything. I made the appointment for the first treatment and then we left his office.

I do remember how happy Mom and Dad were. They were both smiling. They were excited that I was going to try a new type of treatment. I think this gave them hope that there was still another potential solution available, a cure for this incurable disease. I, however, burst into tears. I was a thirty-nine-year-old man sobbing like a baby and hugging my parents. I had never cried in front of my parents before.

Shock treatments! I couldn't believe it. You can't sink any lower on the depression treatment spectrum than shock treatment. And I had hit it.

Later that same Saturday, I went to a black-tie fund-raising dinner at the Ritz-Carlton. It was an event I had committed to months ahead of time that I couldn't get out of. Incredibly, I floated, seemingly effortlessly, from table to table, smiling and laughing at all the right times. As far as anyone knew, I had spent the day relaxing on the golf course. I look back now and wonder how I pulled it off. This was an extreme example, but I had "pulled it off" hundreds of times over the years.

chapter five

WHAT, NO CASSEROLES?

Nobody brings you a casserole when you're having shock treatments. I read that somewhere and thought it was hilarious. And it's true. I didn't tell anyone I was having shock treatments and I don't think my family did either. It was a tightly guarded secret. Don't ask, don't tell, and don't want to know.

My memory surrounding the period in which I received ECT is fragmented. It was the summer of 1998. I was still staying at my parents' home. My dad would drive me to the hospital at 7:00 in the morning, and I was home by 11:00 a.m.

I think I had a series of fifteen treatments. Midway through the series of ECT treatments my family changed psychiatrists. I don't remember a thing about this. All I can say is that my family took me to the best psychiatrist in St. Louis. His endless patience, incredible compassion, and tremendous insight into the disease of depression saved me. The comfort I felt at his unfailing kindness during every session motivated me to work through the pain, stay hopeful, and maintain the will to survive. His knowledge of psycho-pharmaceuticals was always on the cutting edge. I still see him for medication management visits. He keeps me in balance. His low-key, low-pressure approach helped offset the high pressure I was under to "snap out of it." I will never be able to repay him for his kindness.

I took a short medical leave of absence during the last half of the ECT treatments. Apparently in the beginning there were some days when I would have a shock treatment in the morning and return to work in the afternoon. I had a lot of pressure from my family to return to work as soon as possible. Their yardstick for my improvement was my putting on a suit and tie and going to work. They strongly felt that it was not a good idea to sit around the house and do nothing.

The mention of shock treatments (ECT) brings up comparisons with Jack Nicholson's role in the 1979 movie *One Flew Over The Cuckoo's Nest*. Unlike the shock treatments, I would be much more open about telling close friends about my vagus nerve stimulator implant procedure. For whatever reason, I didn't feel anything close to the stigma that was associated with ECT. The physical solution (implant procedure) to a mental health problem carried less of a stigma than electric shocks.

So I returned to work, but much too soon. My first day back I didn't know what day of the week it was or even which floor I worked on. Was it the sixteenth or the seventeenth? I couldn't remember. I was terribly self-conscious and uncomfortable returning to work after an unexplained three-week absence. I am sure it was bizarre for my co-workers. Something happened, but what?

This was another one of those "don't ask, don't tell, don't want to know" situations. I was crushed by the shame and embarrassment of the shock treatments. The cover-up was on in full force.

I made it to my desk, but I couldn't remember how to turn on the computer—let alone how to use it. I sat there for about an hour, shuffling papers from one side of the desk to the other, trying to think of a plan. I was good at masquerading, but I quickly decided I couldn't perform miracles. I knew I had to come clean with someone, because this memory loss wasn't going to improve in one day. Fortunately there was a wonderful woman in the next cubicle named Denise. Denise was and is a saint. I went into her cubicle and quietly explained I needed her help. She never asked one personal question. She took me by the hand, walked into my cubicle, pulled up a chair, and started from square one, saving me from any further embarrassment in the office. Her empathy and genuine kindness were truly extraordinary. She freely gave of her time to get me jump-started. In any event, within a few weeks 80 percent of my memory returned, the other 20 percent never came back.

I don't regret for a minute my decision to have ECT. In fact, there was no doubt I'd do it since there was nothing else left to try. But it didn't work for me. A year or so later my family told me that I looked absolutely horrible during this period.

As my depression worsened in 1998 and 1999, it became harder and harder to learn new tasks, which greatly affected my productivity at work. I kept switching jobs and departments. Every new job or department required learning new tasks. One of my jobs at the bank required me to travel around the country and give the same short talk to groups of three to ten people. I couldn't do it. I practiced the presentation over and over. I would go into an empty conference room and practice out loud. I stayed late at the office, working on this short talk that dealt in the general subject matter I had been trained in for twenty years. When it became clear I couldn't master this little presentation, I switched to a new company. And then, after a month at the new company, I tried to switch to another company that had also given me an offer. They turned me down. I am sure they thought I was nuts.

You might wonder how I could get so many job offers. In short, I was a great interviewer. I wore Brooks Brothers suits, Italian silk ties, and Ferragamo shoes. I could psyche myself up for any opportunity I thought would change my life. I looked good. I sounded good. I gave all the right answers. I could perform brilliantly for a thirty-minute interview. But with severe, chronic depression I couldn't perform effectively on any job.

With each job failure I sank further and further into the bowels of depression. By late 1999, I was a social recluse. The only escape from my misery was sleep. I lived to sleep. I got off work at 5:30 or 6:00 p.m. I would pick up some take-out food for a quick dinner. Then it was bedtime. I was often in bed by 7:00 or 7:30 and I would sleep straight through until 7:00 the next morning if it were a weekday. If it was the weekend, I could sleep fourteen hours straight. I hated the thought of getting out of bed and facing the world. Many sufferers of chronic depression hate mornings. It's an awful feeling.

The late 1990s weren't all work and sleep. I worked hard at clinging to the image that everything in my life was normal. For instance, my friends would invite me out to a movie and dinner. As soon as I was invited, panic would set in. I dreaded it. If I was invited on a Monday for a weekend movie, it was a long week. It's not possible to underestimate how stressful and how much energy it took me to go out for dinner and a movie. We'd see the movie and everyone else would talk about it at dinner. I couldn't concentrate enough to follow the plot, so I would sit in the movie theater for two hours, periodically looking at my watch, having little idea about the movie's main story line or even the names of the main characters. At dinner, I would nod my head periodically, acknowledging some particularly riveting scene that my dinner companions were talking about. And all the time I just wanted to get home as soon as possible, where I felt safe. The need to hide the hopelessness I felt left me feeling more isolated and consequently more depressed.

It was no way to live. I white-knuckled it seven days a week. Finally, thankfully, I couldn't work anymore. I say thankfully because quitting work stopped the downward spiral. I didn't stand a chance of getting better until the bleeding stopped. It was clear to my psychiatrist that I could not continue to work. Even my dad (the last holdout) finally said to me, "You're not going to make it if you don't give yourself a break."

chapter six

Do Not Disturb

I was now entering the third year of a major depres-
sive episode. Isolation and social withdrawal, common symptoms
of chronic depression, were a part of my life on a daily basis.
However, in the normal course of events, there were many challenges to the "do not disturb" plan I had established. I wanted to
perpetuate the appearance that everything was okay by fulfilling as
many of my responsibilities as possible. On the other hand, there
were things I was simply not well enough to do, which meant there
was a constant tug-of-war going on between my outer persona and
the reality of how ill I was inside.

The same week I had to take a medical leave of absence from
work due to absolute physical and mental exhaustion, the battle
was in full force. I received a telephone call from my brother in-
law Russell. He told me he was giving my sister a surprise fortieth
birthday party in December, with sixty or seventy people, at their
home. Hmm. Seventy people crowded into a small living room,
many of whom I had not seen in ten or twenty years, all asking me,

"So, what are you doing now?" It just doesn't get any better than that!

I certainly wanted my sister to have a nice party, so the next day, during my weekly appointment with my psychologist, I threw myself on her mercy. I spent the next two months fretting about this surprise party on the couch in my psychologist's office. I wondered if I could attend the party. What would people think? What would I do? Go for an hour and then leave quietly? Go for half an hour and then excuse myself to go to another commitment? Stay for the entire party? It won't be as stressful as I am projecting it to be, right? Don't go at all? I discussed all these possibilities and everything in between. I felt if I attended the party, everyone would be staring at me and quizzing me about my life.

I did not decide what to do until forty-five minutes before the party. I made a last-minute beer run, blew up some balloons, hugged my brother in-law, and said, "I can't do it." Russell understood. My father concurred. I felt guilty, like a louse. But today I still stand by my decision. People who are ill (mentally or physically) do not belong at festive celebrations. I would share that same advice with anyone. Except . . .

In the summer of 2000 my phone rang with another challenge to my "do not disturb" plan. My dad said my other sister (who had surprisingly eloped with her longtime boyfriend) wanted a big wedding party in the fall, including a couple hundred guests, a band, a sit-down dinner—the whole works. Oh no, here we go again! But this time the choice was clearer; I couldn't NOT go to my sister's wedding party. Meanwhile, back on the psychologist's couch, the doctor had her work cut out for her.

The night of the party I was pumped. I drove to the club; pressed the elevator button for the twenty-third floor, and up I went. Twenty, twenty-one, twenty-two, and then the twenty-third floor. Ding. The doors opened and it was show time. It was a beautiful party, my sister was thrilled, and her friends were terrific. Even I could feel the joy and happiness. I did great, with just a few weak moments sprinkled in. But, man, it was hard work. When everyone was good and drunk, I found the elevator and departed. I felt like Rocky Balboa. I was so elated you could have peeled me off the ceiling. I was happy for my sister and her perfect party, and I gave myself a big pat on the back.

In early March 2001, the phone rang again. This time it was my sister-in-law Mary announcing a surprise fortieth birthday party for my brother. She said it would be great if I came, but no big deal. It was up to me. After the agony surrounding my sister's surprise party I had developed a rigid structure of systematically eliminating all unnecessary stress. I was in survival mode, in complete and utter despair, and I couldn't take it anymore. Sorry Michael, but I was a no-show at your party. He was so shocked by the surprise party, however, I'm sure he didn't notice my absence.

Two weeks after this party, I had the VNS implant procedure. Truly, though at this time in my life I simply wanted to die on the operating table. But as long as I was alive . . . I had to keep grinding away at keeping up the appearance of being a regular person. It was getting old. And I was getting tired.

My rigid structure of systematically eliminating all unnecessary stress was put to the test the next month when another one of my sisters called to say she wanted to throw Mom a surprise sixty-fifth birthday party in June. This was another event I could not imagine skipping. How can you miss your mother's sixty-fifth birthday party? You can't. I did everything in my power to make it as nice a party as possible. Once again, it was hard work to push myself forward while secretly not wanting to live. (My family was clueless as to my true state of mind.)

The party was wonderful. Mom was truly surprised, honored, and very happy to be the cause of this special occasion full of warmth and love. It even made a chronically depressed person happy. The only lesson learned in this situation had nothing to do with depression. It was that you should never plan a surprise birthday party with six siblings, each with conflicting ideas!

I wasn't only attending parties for other people. In 1998 I turned forty and had a party to celebrate. Even in the best of times, I never particularly liked celebrating my birthday. Fortunately this wasn't a surprise party with long-lost friends and acquaintances. It was a private dinner given by my parents at their home and attended only by my immediate and loving family. I remember the party because it was low-key and I was surrounded by the people who cared for me. My mother decorated the dining room table with a fortieth birthday theme. We had a wonderful dinner and a cake with candles, of course. I saved many of the decorations from the party.

Meanwhile, I had gained more than thirty pounds because I was sleeping an average of fourteen hours a day. Eating was one of my only pleasures and I did practically nothing active. I had tried exercising numerous times in the past. I knew it was a proven fact that exercise can elevate mood, and when I was younger I could play a couple of hours of tennis and then go for a run in 90-degree weather. The endorphins would kick in and I felt great. It was an emotional high, and I wanted to regain that feeling.

But no matter how hard and how often I exercised on the Stairmaster™, my mood never improved. No endorphins kicked in. Nothing. In fact, going to a public gym was horrifying. I

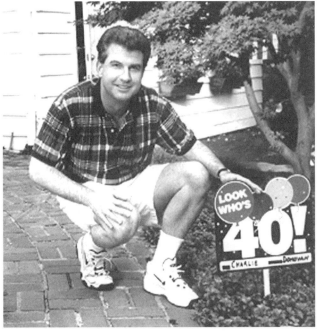

This sign greeted Charlie on his fortieth birthday party, held at his parents' house.

remember walking into the room where the Stairmasters™ were located, scared to death. The walls seemed fifty feet high. I felt panicky, self-conscious, and nervous. Everything about the experience was dismal. But I forced myself to spend thirty minutes on the Stairmaster™ as often as possible because everything I read said that exercise elevates mood.

Exercise did not work for me. I derived absolutely no relief from my depression, so I ultimately threw in the towel.

chapter seven

IT'S A LONG NEW YEAR'S EVE . . .

It's a long New Year's Eve that begins on the Fourth of July. I disliked the Fourth of July for two reasons. First, it reminded me of the fun holiday weekends I used to spend at the beach every summer. In my childhood we would go to Marblehead, Massachusetts, or Cape Cod. And when I was in my twenties I spent time in the Hamptons at the eastern end of Long Island. Secondly, Fourth of July meant the holiday season was fast approaching.

Many people don't particularly enjoy the holiday season. It's almost a cliché to complain about the holidays, but when someone suffers from chronic depression, the time between Thanksgiving and New Year's Eve can be challenging. Although I doubt many people start dreading the holidays in July.

The best time of the year for me was the second week of January. The holidays were over and I had six months before July 4th.

The millennium was ushered in with little fanfare. I was on an

unpaid medical leave of absence from work. I had friends who cel-
ebrated the turn of the century with magnificent trips, parties, and
extravaganzas. I could have cared less. I was in bed by 9:00 p.m.
But most importantly, my boss wasn't beating me up and I wasn't
suffering total mental and physical exhaustion from the daily pressure of trying to learn new material for my latest job change
(August 1999). It was a tremendous relief. The relief far out-
weighed the loss of income. I now had a chance to heal, recover,
and regroup; something that was impossible under all of the stress
I had existed under the previous five years. Quitting work ultimately proved to be the right way to start the twenty-first century.

I recently read an article about phobias. It contained brief
descriptions about cynophobia (fear of dogs), clourophoia (fear of
clowns), and five or six other phobias. I found my phobia, or
rather my former phobia. I never knew it had a name: *agoraphobia*. The article did a great job of explaining phobias. Here is what
it said:

> Phobias may be irrational, but they are also very real.
> Agoraphobia, which is a fear of public places, can rule a vic-
> tim's life. The National Institute of Mental Health estimates
> that 5.1 to 12.5 percent of Americans suffer from phobias.
> Phobias are estimated to be the most common psychiatric ill-
> ness among women of any age, and the second most common
> among men over 25.
>   Agoraphobia is generally interpreted as a fear of public
> places and a fear of being unable to escape the situation. This
> is the most common and the most debilitating phobia. It can
> cripple someone and greatly affect their life.
>
> *St. Louis Post Dispatch*, April 26, 2004

It seems I always have the most debilitating of anything! This
described me perfectly. I was fearful every time I left my home. My
home was my nest. It was where I felt safest. I did not have to
struggle to keep up appearances. Anything that involved leaving
my "nest" was stressful.

Although I live less than two miles from the largest shopping mall in St. Louis, The Galleria, it was the last place I would go to shop. Why? Because it would be the most likely place I would see people I knew and hadn't seen in one, two, five, or ten years. I didn't want to put on a happy face and make small talk. I certainly didn't want to say, "I'm in my third year of a major depressive episode. How are you doing?"

If I needed to go to a mall, I drove fifteen miles from home, minimizing the chance for an unwanted encounter. If I *had* to go to The Galleria for something, I took all the shortcuts and would actually run into the mall, make my purchase, and run out again. My heart would be pounding and I would be sweating because I was so scared. I couldn't get home fast enough.

This pattern was repeated over and over, whether it was the grocery story or the post office. It didn't matter. Anywhere but home was difficult for me.

The best description of me at this time is that I was a mental vegetable, a shut-in. I lived in a prison without bars. I wasn't working. I had no outside interests, no hobbies, and hadn't read a book or seen a movie in a long time. When I did have to engage in social conversation with a friend or a relative who knew about my personal situation, I tried to be empathetic. They were in a difficult situation as well; it's tough having a conversation with the equivalent of a doorknob. But overall, most people were exceedingly gracious and kind to me. Nobody asked intrusive questions, and the conversation was generally kept light. They did everything they could to make me feel comfortable and at ease. I did the same for them. And I continued the charade that everything was hunky dory.

Meanwhile my immediate family wondered what the hell was going on. They were in an impossible situation. As far as they could tell I was fine. I looked good and sounded good, so why wasn't I back to leaping tall buildings? By perpetuating this cover-up, I confused the hell out of everyone and ultimately made life more difficult for myself. The better I tried to look on the outside, the worse I felt on the inside, further baffling everyone around me, and increasing my need to isolate myself.

My family (like the rest of the world) did not understand the disease of depression or, more specifically, chronic depression. They wondered about me constantly. Is he really better? If so, then he needs to get his shit together. Maybe he's not better, now what do we do? Is it live or is it Memorex? They could not comprehend how I could exist the way I was living. They wanted to fix what was broken so that I could live a happy life.

But no one knew what to do. I could go away for a couple of months to a place like The Menninger Clinic in Topeka, Kansas (now in Houston, Texas), or McLean Hospital in Boston. There was an alternative institution in Arizona or New Mexico. But I felt in my gut there was nothing any of these facilities could do for me. My family wanted me to seriously consider this for a solution. I had done a lot of research on the subject, and had a stack of marketing brochures. I came close to entering one of those places, but in the end I didn't and I am convinced it would not have worked.

My family was totally frustrated and confused. I had promised myself I would never lie to my family when asked a question. After a while, however, I started to run out of tactful ways to tell them I was dead from the neck up and in a continuous state of utter despair.

"Oh, I had an uneventful day," I would say.

"And then what did you do after that?" they would ask.

I eventually ran out of answers. How many ways could I tell them I hadn't done anything? I felt like a spin doctor, trying to put my best face on everything.

Social isolation, withdrawal, and loss of interest in the outside world are textbook symptoms of depression. I think my family thought if they encouraged me to get out, attend parties, watch football and hockey games, etc., I would be cured. Wrong!

I am not a mental health professional, but I can say that if you are suffering from severe depression and agoraphobia (fear of public places) there is no worse place to be than a big party or a crowded seventy-thousand seat stadium filled with screaming drunks.

But I did these and other similar things to please my family and friends. I know they meant well, but it is like telling a person with a broken leg to go for a two-mile jog around the track because it will be good for them. It won't help the broken leg to run for two miles, and it doesn't help a depressed person with agoraphobia to go out into public when they are not ready to do so.

I developed a herniated disc two years ago. One simple piece of advice the physical therapist gave me was: "If something doesn't feel good or aggravates the pain in your back, don't do it!" Sadly this common-sense advice is not dispensed to people with a mental illness. I was a people pleaser and I did what other people thought was good for me, no matter how painful it was. Every time I subjected myself to additional mental stress or discomfort, it took me down a notch.

In essence, I felt worthless, guilty, sad, hopeless, and fatigued. I could not concentrate, follow a conversation, or experience pleasure. My misery was unending.

Chronic depression continues without interruption. No one can fix chronic depression, not the doctors, not you. And every-

body gets frustrated. My strategy was to never miss a dose of medication, a psychotherapy appointment, or an appointment with
my psychiatrist. I continued to hope that something would break
my way.

O

chapter eight

A Glimmer of Light

On Tuesday, October 23, 2000, I felt particularly desperate during my regular therapy session with my psychologist. I didn't know what to do. My entire body ached. I sat on the edge of the couch, hands clutched, pleading, "You've just got to help me. What's going to happen to me? What kind of future do I have? How do I get out of this mental hellhole?"

I had been seeing this psychologist for several years; initially on a weekly basis; now every two weeks. I never missed an appointment. My only hope of getting better was to stick to a strict treatment plan. I hoped that maybe I would get a lucky break and get better. I got the first hint of a fluky break that day.

During our session, the psychologist casually mentioned she had recently read something about vagus nerve stimulation and depression in *TIME* or *Newsweek* magazine. (I had never heard of the vagus nerve.) She couldn't remember any of the details from the article. We looked through some magazines in her waiting room, but couldn't find the article. I said I would ask my psychiatrist about it at my next scheduled office visit. Then I went straight to the periodical's section of the local library. After an hour of skimming magazines, I found the article about vagus nerve stimulation and epilepsy. The last sentence of the article casually mentioned that stimulation of the vagus nerve might have some implications for sufferers of chronic depression. Hmm . . .

On Thursday, November 2, 2000, I met with my psychiatrist. As I sat in the waiting room, I thought about all the times over the past couple of years that I had squirmed in my chair, asking myself: "What am I going to say to this guy? It's always doom and gloom." His compassion, patience, understanding of depression, and incredible insight into what was going on in my mind was remarkable. He listened carefully; he didn't talk a lot during a session, but when it was his time to speak, the information was golden. No condescending platitudes; only measured guidance and support. I always left his office feeling encouraged to keep on going. At the end of this visit, I asked him if he had heard anything about vagus nerve stimulation and depression. He told me he had and that St. Louis University (SLU) was going to be involved in the investigational clinical trial.

Ironically, St. Louis University was only ten minutes from where I lived! I was determined to find out more about the clinical trial. There was something about the word *investigational* that implied aggressive to me. I liked the sound of it. If it's aggressive, it must be good. I paid the receptionist and drove home. As soon as I walked in the door, I picked up the phone and dialed 411. I asked for the telephone number for St. Louis University. After a short pause I heard, "Press the number one and the call will be automatically dialed. An additional charge will apply." Who cares? I pressed the number one before the recording could finish.

The university operator had trouble connecting me with anyone who had heard of this procedure. I was passed around from department to department, including one that experimented on rats and mice (I knew I must be getting closer!). Eventually I reached the Department of Psychiatry, and then, finally, the Clinical Trials Unit within the Department of Psychiatry, where I left a message with the receptionist. I wasn't sure whether I had reached a dead end. Miraculously I got a call from a psychiatric nurse, JoAnn Filla Taylor, RN, the next day. She conducted a pre-screening telephone interview to determine if I would be a suitable candidate for the next stage of pre-qualification. She scheduled me for more interviews, including a meeting with the psychiatrist who was the lead investigator for the study at St. Louis University (SLU), Charles F. Conway, MD.

On Monday, November 20, 2000, in the Clinical Trials Unit of the Department of Psychiatry at SLU, I was interviewed by several people; filled out many forms, surveys, and depression rating questionnaires; and provided my medical history, including medications, hospitalizations, and doctors' names and addresses. It was not a simple process; I didn't just walk in the door and say I'd like to volunteer for the investigational clinical trial. I had to qualify to be included as a study patient. And these interviews and questionnaires were only the beginning.

The study investigators had to independently verify each piece of information. They required records from doctors and hospitals going back many years to verify that I had indeed tried all available treatments for depression and that all the treatments had failed. The interviews were unusual. I wasn't sure what type of person they were looking for and they were somewhat vague about exactly what it took to get in. I guess that was part of the study design. It was definitely not like interviewing for a prime-time TV reality show, where you pretty much know what the producers are looking for. I had the feeling they weren't looking for the "Joe Millionaire" type or even "Average Joe," but more like "Joe Defeated." I don't mean to use the word "defeated" in a derogatory manner, rather I use it to describe the losing battle I was experiencing with depression. After all, every available medical therapy (pharmaceuticals, ECT, psychotherapy) had failed me. I also had the sense they wanted someone who was motivated to get better.

The exact criteria for inclusion in the study have not yet been published. However, a summary of the characteristics of the study patients is shown in the following sidebar. These characteristics are derived by using the Hamilton Rating Scale for Depression (see Appendix I). These were patients suffering from an episode of severe depression that had lasted for an average of four years, with a total of twenty-five years of depression over their lifetimes! No other trial ever studied such a severely depressed patient population.

Patient Characteristics in Clinical Trial	Evaluable Population (205 patients)
Average Age(years)	46
% of Female Patients	64%
Average Baseline Depression Rating	Moderate to severe
Average Duration of Lifetime Illness	25
Average Duration, Current Episode (years)	4.2
% Treated with ECT in Current Episode	35%

Reference: Cyberonics Presentation to FDA Advisory Panel on June 15, 2004.

The study was a double-blind placebo-controlled study, which meant I had a 50 percent chance of *not* receiving treatment (stimulation to my vagus nerve) until after I had completed the short-term phase of the study. In a double-blind study, neither the doctors nor patients know who is receiving the treatment. Even though I would be implanted with the device, there was a 50 percent chance it wouldn't be turned on right away, although even patients in the placebo group would eventually have the device turned on. That was the deal. Take it or leave it.

I desperately wanted to know what the odds were of getting relief from my depression. And that's the question they couldn't answer. This was truly a pioneering experimental study, so nobody had the answer. The doctor's response to my question about what were the odds that vagus nerve stimulation could help me was cautious and measured. He said there was an *inkling* there may be something to this.

I said to myself, "*Inkling*? I'll take an inkling. An *inkling* was all I needed to agree to the procedure." I had tried everything else. As long as the procedure was safe, which it is, I had nothing to lose. And I suspect that many desperate patients will feel the same way. But now, people will have the benefit of knowing that vagus nerve stimulation is much more than just an inkling, it has been proven to positively affect the areas of the brain that modulate mood and depression.

I had other questions, too:

Is VNS related in any way to ECT?

No, there is no relationship between ECT and vagus nerve stimulation. ECT induces a grand mal seizure, which alters many chemical aspects of the brain during and after seizure activity.

How big are the scars?

The nurse held up two fingers about an inch apart. (She was off by about two inches.)

What's the downside risk?

It might not work, but I would be no worse off than I was now.

How long is the recovery?

Not very long.

Is there any monetary compensation for being a study patient?
No, there was no financial compensation.

The clinical trial had two hundred patients from twenty different hospitals throughout the United States. If I did the math correctly, that meant only ten patients would be implanted at the St. Louis University study site. This made me nervous. It felt like I was in a competition. I hoped I could I get approved fast enough, before all ten slots had been filled.

Over the next few months, I had more interviews with the study investigators. All of my medical records from psychiatrists and hospitals from the last fifteen years had to be reviewed. Then the waiting game began. I would call JoAnn every couple of weeks to see if I had been approved or qualified. "Nothing has been decided," is all that she was authorized to say. There was nothing I could do to improve my chances of being accepted into the trial study.

My family kept asking me what was going on. Even though nobody knew what the procedure was about, they desperately wanted me to have it done. Since I could get no information from SLU, there was nothing I could tell my family. It was a waiting game.

In early February 2001, I made my regular phone call to JoAnn. She told me that a file from one doctor was missing. That doctor's office said they had sent it, but JoAnn never received it. I was determined to be included as a subject for the clinical trial and was not going to let the U.S. Postal Service screw it up. So I got in the car, drove to the doctor's office, picked up the information, and then hand delivered the sealed envelope to JoAnn. Even after personally handing the envelope to JoAnn, I left her office with absolutely no clue as to whether I would be considered a candidate.

Finally, one day in early March, the phone rang. It was JoAnn. "You're in!" she said. I had no idea what I was in for—but I was in! The SLU study investigators had approved me. My information was forwarded to Cyberonics, the manufacturer of the vagus nerve stimulator, where the researchers had given the final approval for me to be included in the study. I was relieved. I was going to get the chance to try a new treatment that could potentially give me some relief from my chronic despair. That's all I wanted, an opportunity, something to hope for, the possibility of improving the quality of my life. I felt like a high school senior who had just gotten accepted into Princeton after being on the waiting list for four months.

During my regularly scheduled office visit on Tuesday March 19, 2001, I told my psychiatrist I had been accepted into the study. I asked him if he thought I should go ahead with the procedure. There was little to discuss. We spent less than five minutes on the subject. The doctor politely suggested I talk it over with my family. We had reached a point where there was absolutely nothing to lose. I'm sure he was thinking I had better go for it and let the chips fall where they may!

I completed the pre-surgery preliminaries, including a couple of office visits with the neurosurgeon, Dr. Richard Bucholz. The implant procedure was scheduled to take place on April 4, 2001. It would be an inpatient overnight hospital stay. On Monday, April 2, 2001, I completed the final round of tests and questionnaires about my depression and related symptoms. I met with my rater— Raymond Tait, PhD, Director of Clinical Trials in the Department of Psychiatry at SLU—the doctor who would meet with me weekly to assess my depression during the short-term part of the study, which would last twelve weeks. He did not know whether I was assigned to the treatment group or the placebo group.

This meeting was to establish the baseline level of my depression. I won't bore you with the details of the numerous questions I had to answer; but I want you to know how depressed I was. I told Dr. Tait I wanted to die on the operating table. I knew the surgery was simple and there was little chance of anything going wrong, but I hoped something inexplicable would happen. If I died during surgery then all of my problems would be solved--it would be the ultimate escape. (Clearly I had nowhere to go but up from that level of depression.)

I felt incredible pressure in the days leading up to the surgery. I believed that if I didn't wake up completely cured I would once again be considered a failure.

The routine procedure was performed on Wednesday, April 4. It is surgery, performed by surgeons in an operating room. Fortunately I had no physical problems (high blood pressure, diabetes, heart disease, allergies, etc.) to potentially complicate the procedure. (More detailed information about the implant is provided in the appendices.)

You should feel no pressure about having this surgery, in fact just the opposite. Now the researchers know that improvement in mood occurs gradually, over time. Progress should be measured in calendar quarters, not weeks. (I elaborate on this later in the book.)

My parents drove me to the hospital at 6:00 in the morning. We checked in and went to the operating area. I put on a hospital gown, a nurse stuck an IV in me, and my parents and I watched the *Today Show* for an hour and a half. My dad gave me one good piece of advice: make sure you ask for something to calm your nerves before surgery. The anesthesiologist obliged. I hugged my dad. I hugged my mom. I was wheeled away for surgery. My parents left for a sumptuous breakfast in the hospital cafeteria.

In the operating room the Chief Neurosurgery Resident greeted me. The anesthesiologist put me to sleep. A stimulator was implanted in my upper left chest; two lead wires from the stimulator were tunneled under my skin and wrapped around the left vagus nerve in my neck. The surgeon's knife never went above the fold in the lowest part of my neck.

The implant procedure is relatively simple. Surgeons have been doing chest implants since 1958 and this identical procedure has been performed safely on more than 30,000 epilepsy patients since 1997. However, you certainly want the surgeon to pay attention when he coils the lead wire around your vagus nerve!

I strongly recommend that patients choose a surgeon who has specific experience operating within the carotid sheath. The vagus nerve lies deep and in between the common carotid artery and the jugular vein. This is the most critical part of the procedure.

Steven C. Schacter and Dieter Schmidt, Vagus Nerve Stimulation, Second Edition, 2003. Martin Dunitz.

The surgery was uneventful. It was over before lunchtime. My parents and JoAnn were waiting for me. The neurosurgeon told them everything went fine, no problems. My parents tried to find out from JoAnn whether I would be assigned to the treatment group and what was the probability of success. They had no luck in getting an answer from her. I was happy my parents met JoAnn, because they had a chance to pick her brain. They quickly discovered the study investigators were not divulging any information that would compromise the study. People suffering from chronic depression are often accused of keeping secrets. My family thought I had been deliberately withholding information from them. It was nice to have third-party verification I wasn't hiding anything about the treatment. I think my dad summed it up best when he said he couldn't get a thing (information) out of that broad (JoAnn)!

The neurosurgeon stopped by later in the afternoon; while I was being catheterized no less. I saw him a week later for a quick checkup for scars. I haven't seen him since. I wouldn't know what he looked like if I bumped into him on the street. He did a great job. The scars healed beautifully. His job was done.

chapter nine

I'VE BEEN IMPLANTED, NOW WHAT?

You will have many questions when you consider this surgery. Although I had no answers before my surgery; I want you to have the benefit of my experience.

How bad is the pain?

During the twelve hours post surgery I mostly slept, due to the anesthesia. I felt minor soreness and stiffness around the implant. I could definitely feel the implant under the skin of my upper left chest. I was extremely hoarse. My throat was sore from the intubation tube used during surgery. The doctor prescribed Tylenol™ with codeine—none of the good stuff like Vicodin™ or OxyContin™! I needed the pain medication for about three days after the surgery. I kept thinking to myself, I just had surgery, shouldn't I be in more pain? But I wasn't.

What do the scars look like?

Since I didn't have a camera crew waiting for me as I exited the recovery room, I don't have pictures of the fresh scars. But those would be irrelevant.

In the weeks following the surgery, I was surprised by the size of the scar on my neck. It was bigger than I had expected; it was four inches long and swollen. If you're a man and have to shave around the bottom of your neck, you will have to be careful for a month. If you're a woman and you have to shave around the bottom of your neck, I can't help you.

Since I was implanted Cyberonics has introduced a revised model of the stimulator, Model 102, which is 30 percent smaller and has 46 percent less volume than its predecessor. It also has one lead wire rather than two. This means that the procedure should now cause less scarring than I experienced, and the neurosurgeon has only one lead to coil around the vagus nerve. Cyberonics has announced they will have Model 103 available in 2005, a smaller version than Model 102 that offers enhanced functionality for the surgeon as well as increased options for setting the stimulation parameters of the device.

After healing, the scars are minor. I have included several pictures on the following pages, taken by a professional photographer, of the scar on my neck and the scar on my upper left chest. (They say a picture is worth a thousand words, and these pictures should make anyone feel comfortable that he or she could live with this minor scar, even if they derived no benefit whatsoever from the device.

After these pictures were taken, I sent them to my editor, Roxann Schroeder, PhD and to the book packager who would create my book in e-book and paperback formats, Mary Jo Zazueta.

Scar on neck.

Scar on upper left chest.

With a suit and tie on, the scars are unnoticeable.

I wanted to know right away if there would be any issues with the pictures, so we had time to correct the problem before publication. Mary Jo said there must have been trouble with the lighting or the photographer's lense because she could hardly see the scars, especially the one on my upper left chest. However, these pictures are an accurate portrayal of the scars. When I go for a regular physical my primary care physician has difficulty finding the scar on my chest. Since the new stimulators are 30 percent smaller, scars in the future should be even less.

I included the picture of me wearing a tie to show that the scar on the fold of the neck is completely hidden. Roxann pointed out that it would be helpful to have a picture of a woman to show that the scar would not be disfiguring for females either. This brought up another interesting point. One of the rules of the study was we were not allowed to meet or communicate with any other study patient. I have never met or spoken to another patient in the study. So, unless I dressed up in drag, it would be difficult to get a picture of a woman. Sorry about that!

How long does it take to recover?

Not long. I don't remember being given any specific instructions. Obviously, if you still have anesthesia in your system, you shouldn't drive or operate heavy machinery. I have never operated heavy machinery in my life, and I just took it easy for three or four days at my parent's house.

I was still suffering from severe depression. I want to clarify that the post-surgery recovery and the depression recovery are two separate issues.

The meat of the study began on Monday, April 9, five days after the implant. There were two phases to the study, the short-term phase and the long-term phase. The short-term phase was scheduled to last for three months post-surgery. For some patients the short-term phase lasted six months.

Every week for twelve weeks I met with JoAnn. I placed a programmable wand over the area of the implant. The wand was connected to a laptop computer. (Today they use a Palm Pilot.) She pressed a couple of buttons on the computer, the computer made a few noises, then she gave me the okay to put down the wand. This procedure turned off the device for the patients in the treatment group, but the same procedure had to be followed with the placebo group as well, so that no one knew what group he or she was in.

The next step was a two-hour interview and depression-rating session with my rater, Dr. Tait, who also did not know which group I was in. I answered the same questions every week. Even under the best of circumstances this would be a grind, but I had severe hoarseness (more on that later) and no relief from the depression. The interviews became tedious and frustrating.

After our meetings, Dr. Tait would complete a separate questionnaire on his observations about me. I headed back to JoAnn's office, where there was another questionnaire waiting for me. This one I completed by myself in her office. It was a thirty-question multiple-choice questionnaire titled "Inventory of Depressive Symptomatology." Then I placed the programmable wand over the area of the implant. Once again, the computer made a few noises and she would give the signal to put down the wand.

Here is an example of one of the questions in the self-questionnaire, "Inventory of Depressive Symptomatology." Some of the questions were a bit tricky to answer, but this one was always the easiest:

Question 17. View of My Future

___ 0 I have an optimistic view of my future

___ 1 I am occasionally pessimistic about my future, but for the most part I believe things will get better.

___ 2 I am pretty certain that my immediate future (1-2 months) does not hold much promise of good things for me.

___ 3 I see no hope of anything good happening to me any time in the future.

For many months my answer was always the same: #3. I had absolutely no hope about my future. Gradually, my answer changed to #2, and then #1. For the past eighteen months, my answer has been #0. I no longer have to cheat in order to give the answer that I have an optimistic view of my future. (It's a wonderful feeling.)

Then JoAnn got her chance to ask questions. Her job was to monitor any changes in my physical health, medications, and dosages. If I had taken anything new (even Tylenol™) she needed to know the exact date I started the medication and when I discontinued taking it. Did I have any new physical problems? How was the hoarseness? The whole process was meticulous. But, even after all this, I still wasn't done for the day.

The last meeting was always with a psychiatrist. It was a short meeting. He reviewed the information I had given to JoAnn and asked a few questions. By that time, I was more than ready to leave. There was never any variation in the process, the order of the interviews, or the precise nature of the visits. Week after week it was always the same. I stopped counting after a while. I just did what I was told.

Three years after my implant surgery these visits still continue, although only on a quarterly basis. The process is the same, except we skip the sham part of the process, since I have been *unblinded*. I also complete the self-assessment questionnaire every month. JoAnn phones to notify me it's time to do the questionnaire, which we now, thankfully, do over the phone. I do not know the date my stimulator was turned on or how and when it was ramped up to toleration. They say they may never be allowed to tell me. At this point, I don't care. The device proved effective for me, that is all I need to know!

In addition to the main study, there were several optional parts to it. I agreed to give periodic blood samples and to have PET scans. A positron emission tomography (PET) scan is an imaging technique that uses positively charged particles to detect subtle changes in the body's metabolism and chemical activities. It provides a color-coded image of the body's function, rather than its structure. Medical specialists are just beginning to discover how PET scans can be used to evaluate a wide range of patients, including psychiatric patients. I hope my participation in this part of the study was helpful. I did not agree to have my interviews videotaped. No thanks. (This may prove to be a wise decision. I am writing this as Jay Leno is making jokes about Paris Hilton's secret sex video. What if I somehow became rich and famous? You know the tapes would surface. No thank you.)

I was a good patient. I never missed an appointment for blood work, PET scans, interviews, or physicals. I did everything I was told.

Even after a month the hoarseness was not lessening. There was no pain; just severe hoarseness. And every week, the study investigators would nod their heads sympathetically but said nothing. Their silence was deafening. I wanted to know more.

On Tuesday, May 8, 2001, I made an appointment with an Ear, Nose and Throat specialist at Barnes Hospital in St. Louis. "Squeeze this," he said, handing me a ball of gauze. "You might feel some discomfort." He stuck a scope through my nose and down to my throat so that he could see my vocal cords. Whenever a doctor says you may feel some discomfort, you know you're in trouble.

"Your left vocal cord is not moving," he said. After thinking about it for a couple of minutes he said, "I've never heard of this crazy procedure. But if I were you, I would just let Mother Nature take her course. I think over time, you'll be fine." It turns out he gave me good advice.

Little by little, the hoarseness lessened. There was substantial improvement three to four months after the implant, when it was impossible to differentiate the hoarseness from the initial surgery and the hoarseness that resulted from the activation of the stimulator. It is important to note that while some patients have hoarseness or voice alteration from the device activating, these side effects dissipate over time. I have no voice alteration anymore, nor do I feel anything when the stimulator is activated. The only way I know for sure that the device is working is when JoAnn checks the settings.

Less than 1 percent of the patients in the study had temporary left vocal cord paralysis after surgery. I mention it because it happened to me. Hoarseness was a side effect of the surgery in 68 percent of the patients, but it dissipated over time, and the length of time varied with each patient. Meanwhile, the benefits of stimulation kicked in gradually. In my opinion, if you have suffered from chronic depression for many years, then a few months of tolerable side effects should not deter you from considering this procedure.

I don't know when my stimulator was turned on. I learned in November 2003 I was assigned to the treatment group from day one, but because of my severe hoarseness the device was not turned on or ramped up until the hoarseness settled down. I do not know what level the device is currently set at. The study investigators say I may never be told.

At some point (probably late summer 2001) I began to notice a slight tickle in my throat. It was minor and increased the hoarseness a bit. I assumed this was a sign that the stimulator had been activated. The device settings vary with each individual, but a common setting would be thirty seconds of stimulation every five minutes, twenty-four hours a day, seven days a week. The patient does not need to do anything; compliance is guaranteed.

By the late fall, there was minor improvement in my mood. It was subtle, but noticeable.

Wednesday, December 5, 2001, was the day before my regular appointment with my psychiatrist. I remember it distinctly. I carefully laid out the clothes I was going to wear to the appointment. I am sure the doctor thought I owned only one pair of jeans, one shirt, and a pair of tennis shoes. But something inside me wanted me to look good for this appointment. I can't explain it. I found a beautiful cashmere sweater from Saks that I hadn't worn in years, a pair of Italian dress cords, and a starched white shirt. I shined my loafers.

Before depression took over my life, I had taken a lot of pride in the way I dressed. Pulling out nice clothes must sound woefully minor to anyone who has never suffered from chronic depression, but those who suffer can fully appreciate this tiny victory. I told my psychiatrist I lived a quiet, solitary life, which was okay with me. It was not a life most other people would want. But it was an improvement over mental turmoil, which was a huge improvement for me.

The neurosurgeon who performed the implant procedure wanted me to schedule an appointment with him nine months after the surgery, due to the severe hoarseness that was evident a week after the implant. Since the hoarseness eventually improved significantly, I didn't feel like going to another appointment. I was tired of seeing doctors. There would have been little to talk about. On Sunday, January 20, 2002, I wrote him a letter requesting a cancellation of the appointment.

Dr. Bucholz wrote back and agreed an appointment was unnecessary. He also said the hoarseness and scarring would continue to lessen over time.

chapter ten

IF AT FIRST YOU DON'T SUCCEED . . .

On Tuesday, January 22, 2002, Cyberonics, Inc.
issued a significant press release. It is important you fully understand its contents as Cyberonics has never discussed this issue
publicly again—and it has essential implications about the Vagus
Nerve Stimulation Therapy's potential success or failure in
patients. There might be some propaganda and false rumors (via
the internet, uniformed physicians, etc.) about the results of the
short-term part of the study. I have tried to dissect the ramifica-
tions of the press release for you, so you will know and understand
the correct facts.

In any investigational study, whether for a new drug or for a
medical device, there may be mistakes or shortcomings in the
study design. If you are a huge drug company like Merck, with
over $15 billion in annual revenues, these types of oversights don't
become a momentous event and are often hidden from the public.
But if you are a one-product medical device company, with about
$100 million in annual revenues, such events are significant.

PRESS RELEASE

HOUSTON, January 22, 2002 /PRNewswire-FirstCall/ - Cyberonics, Inc. (Nasdaq: CYBX) today announced acute results in the pivotal depression study (D-02) assessing the efficacy of Vagus Nerve Stimulation Therapy (VNS Therapy(TM)) in 235 people with chronic or recurrent depression. There were no statistically significant differences found when 12-week acute treatment and placebo group response and remission rates were compared. A thorough review of all acute data and long-term data is underway. Preliminary review of the treatment group stimulation parameters suggests that over 50% of the patients in the treatment group received insufficient stimulation to derive benefit from VNS Therapy.

"Cyberonics was initially surprised by these acute depression pivotal study results considering the encouraging acute and long-term data from the 60-patient study and the depression mechanism of action findings," commented Robert P. Cummings, Cyberonics' Chairman and Chief Executive Officer. "Our preliminary detailed review of the acute and long-term data from the study suggests that response and remission rates improve over time similar to what was seen in the pilot study, but that inconsistent with our previous epilepsy and depression studies, over 50% of the patients in the treatment group may have been understimulated and did not receive efficacious does of VNS Therapy during the entire 10-week acute treatment period. Our clinical development team led by Richard L. Rudolph, M.D., Vice President of Clinical and Medical Affairs & Chief Medical Officer, is rapidly completing their review of the pivotal study results. At this point, it appears as though we will: 1) request an amendment to the D-02 protocol to require adequate doses of VNS Therapy during the long-term follow-up phase of the study, and 2) request approval to convert our conditionally-approved 550-patient Phase IIIB D-08 protocol into a 300-patient 6-month randomized, double-blind, placebo-controlled confirmatory pivotal study to prove that VNS Therapy is an effective and tolerable long-term maintenance therapy for patients with chronic or recurrent depression."

Dr. Rudolph added, "Although we are disappointed in the acute study results, it is noteworthy that approximately 50% of clinical trials submitted in recent antidepressant New Drug Applications were failed trials. Our preliminary review suggests that the lack of a significant difference between treatment and placebo groups represents a failed study, not a failure of the therapy. We remain confident in the unique value of VNS Therapy as a treatment for depression. Although our depression PMA-S submission may be delayed for two or three years, when it is submitted, it will be supported by compelling long-term clinical evidence that VNS Therapy is an effective and tolerable long-term maintenance therapy which could benefit up to 4 million people with chronic or recurrent depression. The need is still there and the VNS Therapy investigators and patients are still enthusiastic. We expect that we will have FDA approval for our new protocol by June 2002."

# #

Let me clarify what happened, by translating several statements from the press release into plain English.

"Cyberonics today announced acute results in the pivotal depression study assessing the efficacy of Vagus Nerve Stimulation Therapy in 235 people with chronic or recurrent depression."

Translation: *Acute* simply means the short-term part of the study. The twelve-week acute period of the study consisted of three parts: a two-week post-operation recovery period, a two-week period of ramping up the stimulation level, and an eight-week "fixed" level of vagus nerve stimulation.

Pivotal means it is a test to determine if the device works. The purpose of a pivotal trial is to confirm efficacy, patient tolerability, and to monitor adverse reactions. Without efficacy, you can't go to the FDA for approval. Tolerability and adverse reactions information is needed to evaluate the overall benefit-risk relationship of the device and to provide a basis for labeling guidelines (if approved by the FDA). Ironically, safety and tolerability have never been an issue with the device.

To be considered pivotal, a study must:

- Be controlled, using a placebo or a standard therapy as a control condition to compare the treatment results
- Have a double-blind design (neither the patient nor the investigators know if the patient is in the placebo or treatment group) when such a design is practical and ethical. Be randomized—the patients are assigned to the placebo or treatment group randomly
- Be of adequate size--there are enough patients to get a statistically relevant result

A randomized study is not required for medical device investigational trials.

"There were no statistically significant differences found when ten-week acute treatment and placebo group response and remission rates were compared"

Translation: The short-term study failed. *Response* to the device means patients who reported a 50 percent or greater improvement in their depression; *remission* implies a complete recovery.

"A thorough review of all acute (short-term) data and long-term data is underway."

Translation: What the hell went wrong? You can safely assume that there was some sort of turmoil going on at company headquarters. Clearly this was a setback for Cyberonics, but more importantly, it was a major blow to the millions of patients (and their families) that could have benefited from the device.

"Preliminary review of the treatment group stimulation parameters suggests that over 50 percent of the patients in the treatment group received insufficient stimulation to derive benefit from VNS Therapy."

Translation: Apparently the design of the study protocol did not require the investigators at the twenty study sites to ramp up the treatment group patients to an efficacious level of stimulation. Consequently, more than 50 percent of the patients in the treatment group didn't get a therapeutic level of stimulation. "More than 50 percent" could mean 51 percent or it could mean 80 percent. We'll never know.

"Cyberonics was initially surprised by these acute depression pivotal study results considering the encouraging acute and long-term data from the sixty-patient pilot study (from 1998) and the depression mechanism of actions findings."

Translation: *Surprised* was probably the understatement of the year. The patients in the pilot study, as well as thousands of epilepsy patients implanted with the device, had reported an improvement in mood. There was clearly conflicting data in the pivotal study when compared to previous outcomes.

"Our preliminary detailed review of the acute and long-term data from the study suggests that response and remission rates improve over time similar to what was seen in the pilot study; over 50 percent of the patients in the treatment group may have been under-stimulated and did not receive efficacious doses of the VNS Therapy during the entire ten-week acute period."

Translation: The initial design of the study was flawed. This was a pioneering study. Everyone learned important information about how the device works. The acute study failed because patients did not get a therapeutic level of stimulation, but vagus nerve stimulation therapy is not a failure.

"Our preliminary detailed review of the acute and long-term data was similar to what was seen in the pilot studies; over 50 percent of the patients in the treatment group may have been under-stimulated and did not receive efficacious doses of VNS Therapy during the ten-week acute treatment period."

Translation: When the device is first turned on, it is set to 0.25 milliamps, the lowest possible setting. The highest setting is 3.0 milliamps. While the minimum effective level of stimulation has yet to be determined, the best guess is somewhere between 1.0 milliamps and 1.25 milliamps. It turns out that at least 50 percent of the patients in the treatment group had the device turned on, but were never ramped up to an effective level of stimulation. It is like going into a windowless, pitch-black basement and turning on the dimmer switch to the lowest level, then coming back in eight weeks to see if the light has gotten any brighter. It doesn't work that way.

"At this point, it appears as though we will: 1) request an amendment to the D-02* protocol to require adequate doses of therapy during the long-term follow-up phase of the study, and 2)

request approval to convert our conditionally-approved 550-patient Phase IIIB D-08 protocol into a 300-patient 6-month randomized, double-blind, placebo-controlled confirmatory study to prove that VNS Therapy is an effective and tolerable long-term maintenance therapy for patients with chronic or recurrent depression." (D-02 is the official name of the investigational study.)

Translation: This is an important statement for a number of reasons. First of all, it's always a good idea to give patients the correct dosage of therapy. One of the options that Cyberonics was apparently considering was a 550-patient study with a six-month acute period. This would have required 550 chronically depressed people to agree to the implant procedure, knowing they only had a 50 percent chance of having the stimulator turned on for six months. I doubt that would have been easy. Moreover, it was an acknowledgement that it takes time before the patient begins to feel the benefits.

If you think about it logically, what would you rather have: a short-term response (eight weeks) to a treatment or a sustained response that lasted for eight, eighteen, thirty-six or more months? I have experienced a sustained response for almost thirty-six months.

It also highlighted a flaw in the design of the pivotal study, with its eight-week fixed dosage of VNS. On average, the patients in this study had suffered twenty-five years of lifetime depression. Twenty-five years! And the average length of the current episode was 4.1 years. The treatment group patients were given a fixed dose of VNS for eight weeks. Anyone who has suffered chronic depression for twenty-five years, and is in a current depressive episode of

4.1 years, is not going to be cured in eight weeks. That was a completely unreasonable goal. And it contributed to the failed short-term part of the study.

chapter eleven

A Gradual Recovery

On Monday, February 4, 2002, I had my first visit to
SLU following the negative press release discussed in Chapter Ten.
The study investigators didn't mention anything about the failed
acute study. I may have asked them about it, I don't remember. In
any event, this visit was the standard two-hour appointment, and
nothing deviated from any of the previous visits.

I assume the executives at Cyberonics were doing everything
they could to salvage the study and not have to do a complete new
study. And, to their credit, they found a way. Because neurological
devices are considered permanent, the long-term results are considered to be much more important than the short-term results. If a
drug fails the acute portion of a study, it is sent back to the research
lab or completely abandoned. Since the short-term study failed
because a significant number of patients in the treatment group
didn't get an efficacious dose of vagus nerve stimulation, the
answer was quite simple: turn up all the patients to an effective
level of stimulation.

At some point during late winter of 2002, I can imagine the chief executive officer of Cyberonics, Robert "Skip" Cummins, running out of his office and giving the order to turn everybody (the patients) up. Remember the famous scene from the *I Love Lucy Show*, where Lucy and Ethel take a job at a candy factory? The female foreman comes into the room where Lucy and Ethel are working behind a slow moving conveyer belt and she loudly shouts, "Speed it up!" That's probably a good analogy to what was going on at Cyberonics.

My next scheduled visit at SLU was Wednesday, March 6, 2002. Although I was never told I was going to have the level of stimulation increased, there's no doubt in my mind I left SLU that day at a higher setting than when I arrived. The only side effect I felt from the higher setting was a small tickle in my throat and a slight increase in hoarseness when the stimulator switched on. It was minor and easily tolerated. (I should point out that for the past year and a half I haven't felt a thing when the stimulator is activated. Virtually all of the hoarseness has disappeared.)

Thursday, March 7, 2002, was my next scheduled visit with my psychiatrist. I reiterated to the doctor that I lived a quiet life, which was okay with me. Okay is a relative term. "Normal" people would be completely unsatisfied with my "okay" life. But they have never lived in chronic mental anguish. I told the doctor there was a small uptick in my mood. This was a positive and I would take anything I could get. I still lived an isolated life, completely devoid of any social activity.

I started to become concerned about how I could make a living, while still satisfying my need to be isolated. My IRA definitely wasn't increasing in value and a comfortable retirement sitting on the beach was not in the cards. I certainly couldn't be the outgoing salesperson I had been in my prior life. It was impossible. I didn't like to leave my home, let alone make sales calls. I was also apprehensive about falling behind in my computer skills. The whole world was changing while I remained secluded in my condominium.

I developed an interest in the amazing concept of eBay. The fact I developed an interest in anything was remarkable. In the spring of 2002 I taught myself how to sell on eBay, then took an on-line course to learn more. I attended the very first eBay Live in June 2002 in Anaheim, California. It was great to attend the eBay Conference with five thousand other people and be totally anonymous. It was emancipating. I could relax among strangers. I was able to observe firsthand that eBay was a first-class organization and not a giant flea market.

My family, however, was appalled at my involvement in eBay. Even though I never made a dime selling on eBay, the experience was priceless. It jump-started me into doing something productive. And most importantly, it was clear the benefits of continuous vagus nerve stimulation were gradually "kicking in."

And, ultimately, eBay's tremendous success would prove my family wrong. eBay now has a market value in excess of $50 billion and, with its 110 million registered users; eBay would rank as the twelfth most populous nation in the world!

The difficulty about a therapy that works gradually is there is no cataclysmic epiphany that can be identified as the catalyst that changed everything. I had four oars in the water: vagus nerve stimulation, antidepressants, a psychiatrist, and a psychologist. Continuous stimulation of my vagus nerve slowly but surely improved my depression. The therapy had a domino affect. The antidepressants became more effective, further improving the depression, which made the psychotherapy sessions more insightful, which increased my activity level. I wasn't swinging from the chandeliers at any parties, but my foot was in the water.

I think psychotherapy is beneficial. I can't imagine my recovery without the help from my psychologist (PhD), who was and is an amazing therapist with ESP. Incredibly accurate ESP. Within the first sixty seconds of a visit, she can accurately diagnose how well I slept the night before and how I've felt since my last visit. She evaluates the way I walk into her office, how I sit on the couch, and the way I hold my hands. She gives me a quick once-over and then focuses on my face and eyes. That's it. The remaining fifty-nine minutes of the session she continues to peel the onion back.

I cannot understand why any patient who benefits from their treatment plan (medications, therapy, etc.) stops adhering to the plan. Patient compliance is a problem in all areas of medicine, but that was the one issue I had total control over. Taking a few pills a day is simple; it is absolutely confounding to me that 50 percent of patients stop taking their medications. I never missed an office visit or one dose of medication. Yes, I have side effects from my medications, but they are tolerable when compared to the alternative: misery. If I had a chance to get better, it required 100 percent compliance. This was not something I was going to skip, ever.

As my depression improved, I kept telling her I was in uncharted waters; I didn't know what or how to think about what was going on. I was extremely cautious because I felt the improvement in my mood was fragile. I still hadn't gotten my sea legs back. It was also not a straight-line improvement. Charted on a graph, my improvement would look more like the teeth of an upward sloping handsaw. There were setbacks and bounce backs. My psychologist helped guide me through the ever-changing developments in my depression.

You might wonder why I needed therapy if my depression was improving. The best analogy I can make is the ads that appear in the *New York Times Magazine* for high net worth clients with a minimum account size of $25 million. There's usually a picture of a serious looking "advisor" and the text states: "Wealth carries a tremendous burden and responsibility, which requires expert advice." I read these ads and wonder who are these people burdened with $25 million and looking for help? Mental health is a priceless asset that you want to protect, especially after you've lost it and are getting it back.

I was protective of any improvement, so I maintained a "bunker" mentality for a long time. And it was the correct thing to do. Psychotherapy helped me understand the social and psychological factors that contributed to my depression. And it also helped me figure out what kind of life I wanted to live after escaping from the black hole.

Over time, people develop ways of coping with their depression. What does one do when those coping mechanisms are no longer needed? Most people are afraid of change, even if it's a positive change. It helps to have someone guide you through this newly found territory. As you feel better, you also become more aware of the things in your life that are troublesome or that negatively affected you. Depressed people avoid conflict and withdraw from situations that involve conflict. A whole new set of skills are needed to assert yourself and find your place among the people who are close to you once the depression is over.

chapter twelve

Is It Over?

Nobody rings a bell when it's over, if it's over. By October 2003 I was telling my family how much I was looking forward to a great Thanksgiving since I was feeling so much better than I had for many years. Instead of dreading the holidays I was looking forward to a nice Thanksgiving dinner at a club with my immediate family.

Hold on cowboy, not so fast! Family dynamics set me way back by Thanksgiving and Christmas. The details are not important, but I was so disappointed in Thanksgiving, and deathly afraid many of my recent mental health gains had been lost forever. I was hurt and angry. What was the point of shock treatments, countless therapy sessions, thousands of pills, and vagus nerve implant surgery if one's family screws it up again? I was back in the dumper, mad as hell, and scared.

Apparently this was reflected in my visit to SLU on January 14, 2003. This was the most unusual visit I had ever had at SLU. After the routine interviews and questionnaires were finished, my last stop (as usual) was with JoAnn. She asked me something different. "Do you want me to turn up the level of stimulation?"

I was shocked, but I immediately replied, "Absolutely yes. As fast as you can." I placed the programmable wand over the stimulator and less than thirty seconds later the settings were increased. For about a minute I felt a slight tickle in my throat—and that was it. I got in my car and went home.

Over the next month or so, I was back on track again. I was relieved, but it reinforced in my mind that the boogie monster (depression) could rear its ugly head at any moment. I became even more cautious and protective, like a mother bear guarding her cubs. When you have depression, rightly or wrongly, you lose your credibility and you lose respect. And you have to fight to get it back. I fought. It can get ugly. Anyone or anything that posed a threat to me got kicked in the balls. I can practically hear my family saying, "We just don't know what to say to him, he's so sensitive." Enough said!

This is another instance when the guidance of a good therapist is critical as you recover. Everything is changing; your family relationships, friendships, outside activities, etc. There's much that needs to be managed and I looked to my psychologist to guide me through the transformation from utter despair and isolation to spreading my wings little by little.

In the Helpful Resources section of my Web Site, www.vagus-nerve-stimulator.com, I recommend an outstanding book, *Understanding Depression*, by J. Raymond DePaulo, Jr., MD who is the Chairman of the Department of Psychiatry at the Johns Hopkins School of Medicine. It is by far the best book about the disease of depression that is available. There's a lot of self-help junk out there. If you suffer from depression (or have a loved one who does), this book is indispensable. He best describes, in one paragraph, the next six months of my recovery.

"So why does it take so long between the time the symptoms go away and when you feel back to normal? (Some patients never completely get back to normal.) What usually happens first is you begin to look better. You are no longer "leaning into the wind"—your posture is better, you move with more agility, your skin tone and color are better, and you speak more animatedly. You begin to regain some of the vitality and energy you lost when you were depressed. Yet if you were my patient and I told you that you were looking better, you'd probably think I was out of my mind. When I was a young psychiatrist and didn't realize how differently they were seeing their situation, I would comment on how much better they looked. They insisted that I was mistaken and that I was just trying to encourage them because they knew they certainly didn't *feel* any better. They were perfectly accurate about how they felt, of course, but so was I about my observation (albeit not perfectly). That's because physical improvement regularly occurs before psychological improvement. I always tell patients, "You'll look better before you feel better." The inner symptoms of hopelessness and low self-esteem take more time to recover than vitality and physical condition. Now, I just tell my patients that I've noticed that they seem to have more energy and point out that this is usually the harbinger of things to come . . ."

J. Raymond DePaulo, Jr., MD, *Understanding Depression*

I would add to Dr. DePaulo's comments that the lagging of my "inner symptoms of hopelessness" compared to my physical condition only further contributed to the confusion my family and friends felt about me. Because I looked better, they expected more than I could deliver. We didn't need any additional confusion in this situation. I felt added pressure, until finally I took off the gloves and said that's it. I have had enough. I am going to do what my professional mental health advisors and I think is right for me. I don't care what anybody else thinks. I was dead serious and I meant it. It was incredibly emancipating and ultimately accelerated my recovery.

If I had to describe the next six months, I would say that I adopted Greyhound Bus Line's strategy—"Sit back and leave the driving to us." The device was set to deliver stimulation to the vagus nerve on a regular basis. I was clearly deriving benefits from the habitual, preset stimulation of the vagus nerve, but there was nothing for me to do as a patient. Scientists now know that vagus nerve stimulation efficacy is a function of dosage (level and frequency of stimulation) and time. Perhaps I could have asked the study investigators to increase the level of stimulation to speed things along. I don't know how to best explain this clinical trial, but it was like vagus nerve stimulation boot camp.

The investigators are wonderful people and I enjoy a great relationship with all of them, but as a study patient I couldn't ask for anything (of course, if there were ever any problems, they were accessible 24/7). It was their study and they called the shots. The visits were routine and identical. There wasn't any two-way (between patient and investigator) stimulation strategy. When the programmable wand was placed over the stimulator I had no idea what, if anything, was taking place. By this time I had been well trained not to ask because they couldn't and wouldn't answer.

Mentally, things were improving; but physically I had deteriorated. I had developed a herniated disc and gained thirty-three pounds, as well as four-and-a-half inches around my waist. I was in chronic excruciating pain. Greyhound Bus strategy would not help my physical condition. But eventually I had the motivation, drive, and more importantly had lost the fear (agoraphobia), so I could go to the gym and exercise. I lost the weight between February and August of 2003, but I was not getting significant pain relief. I had to take pain pills on a daily basis. I tried everything to relieve the pain; physical therapy twice a week, physical therapy exercises five to six days a week, weekly sixty-minute back massages, Eastern acupuncture, chiropractors, and pain specialists. I considered going to an Islamic religious healer. I did go to a sacrocranial massage therapist—the treatment was part massage and part psychotherapy. After our first ninety-minute session, she told me that the cause of my pain was my inner child crying in my sacrum. (Oh, really? Well, that may be true, but I'm getting out of here! I want pain relief. My inner child will just have to wait.) I tried everything I could think of because back surgery was absolutely the last option.

In the end I was swimming three or four days a week, had private pilates sessions two days a week, and had thirty minutes of pelvic/lower back traction four times a week. There was still no significant relief from the pain. Finally, I was referred to an incredible medical doctor who specialized in pain resulting from injuries. She was much more than just an expert in pain; she was also a board certified anesthesiologist with special accredited training in rehabilitation in the treatment of injuries and pain. Her approach to pain relief was unlike any I had ever seen before. She focused on the integration of the physical anatomy, injury physiology, physical and structural changes, and their effects on pain. She worked side-by-side with a highly skilled physical therapist. I walked into the exam room and told her that I had tried absolutely everything, and had even lost thirty-three pounds. She said she hated me (jokingly), and then the doctor and her physical therapist did the most thorough, most unusual, and most complete physical exam I had ever had.

After the exam she said two things that shocked me. First she said my body felt like it had rigor mortis and second she was positive she could help me. Rigor mortis? I had felt mentally dead, but my body was still functioning, and I was very active physically. She told me I was as tight as a drum, and there were parts of my body that weren't moving at all. That meant the rest of my body had to compensate, and that was what was causing the pain.

Moshe Feldenkrais, author of the books *Functional Integration* and *Awareness through Movement* best describes my condition in his books when he says the body carries with it all of life's experiences, good and bad. My body carried a whole lot from the years of depression. I had a series of trigger point injections (over three months) that were strategically given in various muscles of my body. The injections caused the tight muscles to spasm and release. I felt pain relief within twenty-four hours of each injection. It was another life-altering event in a life full of altering events.

Dr. John Sarno of NYU's Medical Center Rusk Institute of Rehabilitation did a study several years ago of ninety patients suffering from back pain. He discovered that depression was the cause of the pain in almost half the patients. The cover of the April 26, 2004 issue of *Newsweek* magazine featured a story titled "Treating Back Pain." Although the article was about the 65 million Americans with back pain, there were at least fifteen references to an emotional or mental health issue (depression, anxiety, etc.). The problem of co-morbidity is just beginning to be studied and will hopefully be a catalyst for treating the mental health of the patient, which will help with many of the patient's other healthcare issues. The total cost of back pain in the United States is estimated to be $100 billion annually and the cost of depression is estimated at $80 billion.

I still do pilates, physical therapy, and swimming on a weekly basis, and there are parts of my body that are moving for the first time in many years. The mental illness of depression literally

Weekly sessions of pilates has helped heal some of the physical damage due to years of chronic depression.

destroyed my physical body. Every time I forced myself to do what other people wanted me to do, my body tightened up. The tight muscles did not get enough blood, so the muscles did not get the oxygen they needed. Over many years I had done countless things that other people thought were good for me, and I paid a physical price. The great news is that the physical pain is steadily getting less, but if I slack off for a week or two the pain returns. I am fully committed to maintaining the physical part of my recovery. The mental and physical problems are related; the physical damage resulted from a long life of mental illness (depression).

chapter thirteen

FIRST YOU HUM TO THE MUSIC

My depression and mood continued to improve for the remainder of the year. Researchers now know that mood and depression can continue to improve for up to two years AFTER the patient has been ramped up to an efficacious dose of stimulation. I still wake up every morning asking myself, "Is it (the depression) back?" By the time I get in the shower the answer is the same: no. I am much less suspicious of the improvement in my depression now than I was a year ago. I used to drive by myself in a car for hours, in dead silence. Now, I drive with the radio blaring or with a CD playing, singing to the music and moving to the beat.

Because my mood improvement was gradual there was no epiphany, the most remarkable thing about this treatment is the staying power of the therapy. It's like the Energizer™ bunny; it keeps on going and going. Things keep getting better and better. Any sadness I experience is a normal emotion that anyone would have in response to a negative event. But unlike when I was in the throes of depression, my mood eventually brightens to a normal level.

My wobbly sea legs have gotten stronger and I have become more and more confident. I am not afraid to go to a shopping mall, nor do I have to race through the aisles of the grocery store. Last weekend I attended a small dinner party hosted by someone I had not seen or talked to in over five years. A year ago I never would have considered attending, but then again, I wouldn't have been invited. The friends I lost touch with would have been uncertain about me and whether a dinner invitation would have been appropriate. I ran into this friend at a wake and I assume he could see from the way I acted that I had regained much of my confidence and swagger back. I think it gave him the assurance that it was okay to invite me to his dinner party.

I am also more engaged in life. I hired a Webmaster to help me start a Web Site, vagus-nerve-stimulator.com, which was launched in February 2004. Finding a Webmaster to create a mental health Web Site was an interesting process since nobody wanted to have anything to do with creating a mental health Web Site. My idea sounded crazy. Porn, gambling, or a site promoting illegal drugs from overseas would have been easier to start than a site on mental illness.

One Webmaster I contacted wanted to name the site "cure-my-depression-now.com." Can you imagine anyone recommending a similar name for a physical illness? How about "cure-my-cancer-now.com?" While a name like that would be considered inhumane for a physical illness, the same standard does not apply to mental illnesses. It's not fair, but it is life.

Finally, I discovered a wonderful Webmaster from Montreal, Marc Deschamps. He has been with me from the beginning. He is ethical, loyal and has taken a personal interest in the success of the site and newsletter. I wanted my Web Site to be an information source for sufferers of chronic or treatment-resistant depression. All of the articles are written by mental health professionals and nationally recognized mental health organizations. I am pleased with the high quality of the content. I also wanted the site to be an introduction to vagus nerve stimulation since it is a potential breakthrough medical device for the treatment of chronic depression. Although the outcome and timing of the FDA's approval was uncertain, vagus nerve stimulation sounded like voodoo medicine and it needed to be demystified.

I decided to write this book about my personal battle with depression, my participation in the investigational clinical trial, and the miraculous rebound in my depression due to the stimulator. I hope my story helps you. I am absolutely overwhelmed with gratitude by the powerful recovery that I have experienced. I thought I was a goner, with the next forty-five years of my life stuck in utter despair.

There has been an almost complete turnaround in my life. Right now I am "integrating"—that's the term mental health professionals use to describe this part of my recovery. When someone has been acutely ill for such a long time, every part of the recovery takes longer, including integrating. I had a huge chunk taken out of my life. I lost a lot of time. I am so humbled by the joy and happiness I am now able to experience. I don't have to keep up appearances any more. I love looking at the blooming dogwood trees, colorful azaleas, and smelling the fresh spring air. The Fourth of July is no longer the harbinger of doom and gloom and the upcoming holiday season. If you could package the way I feel now and put a ribbon around it, I'd take it. I don't want or need anything more. If you have your health (physical and mental), a good family, a couple of close friends, and food on the table, you have everything. (Well almost everything—it's time that I restart building that "IRA" thing.)

Thank you for reading my story. The remainder of the book is mostly technical, but it has useful information about vagus nerve stimulation. Vagus nerve stimulation *will* become a mainstream therapy for chronic or treatment-resistant depression.

I wish you the best of luck. May you be as lucky as me.

EPILOGUE

Many authors who write memoirs about a disease they have or a challenge they've overcome conclude their stories by saying they are glad to have suffered and grateful for what they learned from the experience. I am not in any way grateful for my experience. Chronic depression is gruesome beyond words. It is pure hell. Instead, I will end this book the way I began it, with the *Larry King Show*.

As I write this epilogue, former President Bill Clinton (fellow Georgetown University alumnus and commencement speaker at my graduation in May 1980) is being interviewed by Mr. King about his 956-page memoir, *My Life*. Incredibly almost fifteen minutes of the program is devoted to the subject of depression.

I am amazed. A man who was president of the most powerful country in the world for eight years has tremendous insight into the horrifying disease of depression. He simply said some people can be helped with their depression and some can't—and there's nothing to explain the disparity. Outside the mental health community, there are few people who say and actually believe this to be true.

President Clinton's grasp of this baffling disease is remarkable. He talked about a former roommate of his who committed suicide; and the suicide of the Chief of Naval Operations during his administration, Admiral Mike Boorda. Boorda was found at home with a gunshot wound to the chest, a gun found nearby. Clinton praised the admiral as being the sailor's sailor and that he was the first enlisted man in the history of the country to rise to become chief of naval operations.

Of course he talked about the suicide of Vince Foster, deputy White House counsel during the Clinton administration. Clearly pained, the former president explained how he and Vince had been friends in Arkansas, since the ages of four and six. Vince suffered from depression, was under tremendous pressure, and he was being crucified in the press about Travelgate and Whitewatergate. He knew Vince was upset by a particular article published in the *Wall Street Journal* Op-Ed page about him; so he called Vince that night and invited him over to watch a movie, just as they had done many times as kids. Vince declined and said he just wanted to spend some time with his wife, Lisa. President Clinton said that, in retrospect, he was convinced Vince had already decided to commit suicide. The next day Vince shot himself through the back of his head.

After watching the show, I became extremely concerned about a close friend who suffers from terrible depression, including suicidal thoughts. She hadn't returned any of my phone calls in over a week. I drove over to her house the next day to make sure everything was okay. I walked in the door and, while I was extremely relieved to see her, I was visibly shaken. There I was, staring directly into the black hole—and it was scary. "I am doing just fine," she mumbled. I stayed for a few minutes and then drove back home, my heart pounding. I was terrified for her safety.

I called her as soon as I walked into my condominium. I pleaded with her to call me if she seriously contemplated acting upon her suicidal thoughts. I felt totally helpless. She didn't say anything. She could have said, "Yeah, I'll be sure to give you a ring right before I blow my brains out." But she spared me the embarrassment. I felt stupid, but what else could I have done?

Having been sufficiently humbled and reminded that I do not have qualifications in psychotherapy, I have set a much more modest goal for myself. I don't want to ever have to write the sequel to this book: *Return to The Black Hole.*

WRITTEN ON JULY 4, 2004

appendix a

ABOUT CYBERONICS, INC.

Cyberonics is not a start-up company; it has been in business since 1987 and has spent over $130,000,000 to research and develop just one product: the VNS Therapy System™. Cyberonics is profitable and has over $63 million in cash on its balance sheet and has no long-term debt. Cyberonics has a market value of over $500,000,000.

Since its founding in 1987, Cyberonics has safely implanted more than 30,000 epilepsy patients with the vagus nerve stimulator. The VNS Therapy System™ is now considered a mainstream treatment for pharmaco-resistant epilepsy.

In the investigational trials for epilepsy in the mid-1990s, the study investigators noticed many of the patients were reporting an improvement in mood. This unintended benefit was the catalyst for a small pilot study (59 patients) to further investigate vagus nerve stimulation for people suffering from depression. Based on the encouraging results from the pilot study, Cyberonics took the next step and designed the FDA-approved protocol for a 200-patient, double-blind, placebo-controlled study.

On August 20, 2004, Advance Neuromodulation Systems, Inc. announced it had purchased 3.5 million shares of Cyberonics on the open market at a cost of $49,000,000 and is now the largest shareholder of Cyberonics (14.9%). Advanced Neuromodulation Systems, Inc. (ANSI), designs, develops, manufactures, and markets advanced implantable neuromodulation devices that improve the quality of life for people suffering from chronic pain. Neuromodulation devices include implantable neurostimulation devices, which deliver electric current directly to targeted nerves, and implantable drug pumps, which deliver small precisely controlled doses of drugs directly to targeted sites within the body.

Cyberonics' second largest shareholder is Boston Scientific Corporation, a medical device company with over $4 billion in annual sales. Last year, Boston Scientific purchased 3.4 million shares of Cyberonics in the open market and owns 14.8% of Cyberonics. It is extraordinary that these two leaders in medical device therapy truly recognize the value of Cyberonics' VNS Therapy System™ franchise, intellectual property, demand creation organization and model, profitable epilepsy business, and depression indication opportunity.

Other large traditional institutional investors include Fidelity Investments, Massachusetts Financial Services, and John Hancock Funds.

Cyberonics now employs over 500 people. Its European subsidiary (Cyberonics Europe S.A.) is based in Belgium. In addition to Canada, the company has medical consultants in Germany, France, Belgium, and the United Kingdom marketing the VNS Therapy System. Cyberonics is headquartered in Houston, Texas:

Cyberonics, Inc., The Cyberonics Building
100 Cyberonics Boulevard
Houston, Texas 77058
Telephone: 1 (888) VNS-STIM or 1-888-867-7846

If you are interested in VNS Therapy™, I encourage you to telephone the company directly and ask for extension 7330. You will be able to speak with someone in the Clinical Technical Department who can provide you with the most up-to-date information regarding the status of VNS Therapy™. They also will be able to direct you to a psychiatrist and/or surgeon in your area that is familiar with the procedure.

Full disclosure: I am not a shareholder of Cyberonics.

appendix b

What is Vagus Nerve Stimulation?

Vagus Nerve Stimulation (VNS) is not brain surgery, although it is a treatment that affects the function of the brain. Vagus nerve stimulation uses specific stimulation of the vagus nerve to send stimulation to specific parts of the brain that are involved in mood. It is not like Electro-Convulsive Therapy (ECT), a treatment that involves stimulation of the entire brain and induces convulsions in patients.

In fact, patients may not even feel the stimulation from VNS since the vagus nerve does not have the types of nerves that carry pain signals. Nor does VNS interfere with drugs, thus patients having VNS therapy can continue taking their medications without worrying about side effects or interactions between drugs.

What is the vagus nerve?

Vagus means "wandering" in Latin, and is the perfect description for the vagus nerve, the longest nerve in the body. It averages almost two feet in length and "wanders" throughout the upper body. The vagus nerve starts in the brain, goes down the neck, and into the body where it affects the vocal cords, the acid content of the stomach, the heart, the lungs, and other organs. In the brain it projects to areas believed to be responsible for seizures, mood, appetite, memory, and anxiety.[1] However, the vagus nerve cord does not have many pain nerves, so stimulation of the vagus nerve is not painful, although some patients may feel some sensation when electrical pulses are generated.

The history of vagus nerve stimulation

Vagus nerve stimulation has been used to treat epilepsy patients for years; the first human clinical trial was in 1988,[2] and the FDA approved VNS therapy for epilepsy in 1997.[3] So far over 30,000 people worldwide have had VNS therapy, and it has proven to be a safe and effective treatment for epilepsy.[4] These patients have reported minimal side effects, which have tended to decrease over time. The efficacy of the treatment has also been shown to increase with longer treatment time.[5]

When Vagus Nerve Stimulation was first approved for epilepsy, some patients reported an improvement in mood. Researchers decided to design a study specifically to measure changes in a patient's mood and depression due to stimulation of the vagus nerve. In 1999, scientists began the first open label (no placebo group) study for depression with 60 patients. This first study found that there was indeed an improvement in mood for depressed patients. Based on this study, a more detailed and thorough study was designed to determine if vagus nerve stimulation would be a safe, tolerable, and effective treatment for chronic depression.

The completed one-year, double-blind, placebo controlled trial had 235 patients from twenty-one participating hospitals in the United States, and showed clinically significant improvements due to treatment compared to baseline.[6] The acute (short-term) phase lasted three months, during which half of the patients received stimulation (treatment group) and half did not (control group).

The long-term phase of the study lasted an additional nine months (for one year total treatment) of stimulation. The HRSD-24 (24 item clinician-rated Hamilton Rating Scale for Depression) improvements observed over the first year were highly significant. The results of this long-term, pivotal study were submitted to the FDA in October 2003; the FDA's Medical Devices Advisory Panel recommended approval of VNS for chronic depression on June 15, 2004. Of note, Vagus Nerve Stimulation therapy was approved for use in patients with treatment-resistant depression in the European Union in March 2001, and in Canada in April 2001.[7]

How does VNS therapy work?

The Pulse Generator (battery) delivers a small amount of electrical current to the vagus nerve intermittently (thirty seconds on and five minutes off) twenty-four hours a day, seven days a week for up to ten years.[8] The stimulation is delivered automatically, so the patient does not have to do anything. Because there is nothing to remember, compliance is assured. The stimulation is not supposed to be uncomfortable; some patients do not even feel it. A nurse at the doctor's office can adjust the level of stimulation (amount of electricity delivered) if the patient ever feels uncomfortable. In the study reviewed by the FDA, researchers noted several similarities between epileptic and depressed patients.[9]

One of the most important similarities is that VNS treatment efficacy improves *over time*. The *longer* the patient receives stimulation, the *better* the results. In addition, both populations of patients share the following:

- Assured adherence to treatment regimen
- Safety of the procedure
- Safety of the therapy
- High continuation rates
- No drug interactions
- No cognitive impairment (memory loss)

What is the surgery like?

Vagus nerve stimulation is NOT brain surgery, even though it is an invasive surgical procedure that changes the function of the brain. The stimulator is a pacemaker-like device that generates electrical pulses (Pulse Generator); it is implanted under the skin in the left chest through a small incision. While this may sound like a dangerous procedure, it is not. The FDA has approved the use and confirmed the safety of this procedure. More than 30,000 patients have received the implant to treat epilepsy. The vagus nerve stimulation surgery involves two small incisions, one in the chest and one at the lowest part of the neck. At no time does the surgeon physically manipulate the brain.

The surgery to implant the VNS System takes forty-five minutes to two hours. Local, regional, or general anesthesia (putting the patient to sleep) is used during the surgery; the doctor and anesthetist determine which type of anesthesia is best for each patient. Most VNS patients will have outpatient surgery, but some patients may need to stay in the hospital overnight, and in that case they will need a family member or companion to take them home from the hospital.[10]

What happens after the VNS surgery?

Most VNS patients go home the same day or the next day. You will feel some minor stiffness/soreness around the area of the implant for a few days. Your doctor may prescribe a minor pain medication such as Tylenol™ with codeine. A week later your surgeon will probably want to check the scars and a nurse can program/change the settings on the stimulator in the doctor's office.

What are the most common side effects?

Hoarseness is the most common side effect from the stimulation, which is what I experienced. Over time, my hoarseness dissipated and is now virtually unnoticeable. Patient experience indicates that, as a rule, side effects become less noticeable over time and typically do not result in patients discontinuing the therapy.

Obviously if it is determined that you ultimately are deriving no benefit from the stimulation, the Pulse Generator can be turned off. If you are benefiting from stimulation, however, the side effects are minor and tolerable. Any improvement in your depression can be life-changing.

According to Cyberonics' presentation to the FDA Panel on June 15, 2004, the most common side effects reported after the first year of stimulation are:

Voice alteration	56%
Increased cough	6%
Shortness of breath	16%
Neck pain	13%
Sore throat	5%
Tingling	4%
Nausea	2%
Incision pain	6%

Is the VNS surgery final?

The vagus nerve stimulator can be turned off or removed (explanted) at any time if the patient feels it is not helping, or in the unlikely event the patient can't tolerate the stimulation. The device can be completely turned off in less than thirty seconds in the doctor's office. All it requires is for a nurse to hold a programmable wand over the skin above the Pulse Generator.

Explantation (removal) of the vagus nerve stimulation device is possible, however, less than one half of one percent of the 30,000 patients have elected to have the device removed. Just like implantation, the surgery to remove the device is a simple procedure. Only the Pulse Generator is taken out of the body; attempting to remove the electrode from around the vagus nerve could cause damage, and is not recommended.

The Cyberonics Magnet can be used to stop the stimulation. This particular model can clip onto your belt.

The Cyberonics Magnet

Cyberonics will provide you with the Magnet before the implant procedure At any time, you can stop the stimulation with the Cyberonics Magnet. The Magnet can be used to stop the stimulation temporarily or to turn off the Generator. I never had to use the Magnet and my understanding is that few patients needed the Magnet. But, if you plan to sing or speak publicly and if the stimulation bothers you, the Magnet may be useful to you. You simply place the Magnet over the area of the Pulse Generator, and the stimulation will be stopped. When the Magnet is removed, the VNS Therapy System™ is turned back on.

Notes

1. Vagus Nerve Stimulation Therapy Mechanisms of Action. September 24, 2003 presentation by M.S. George, MD. Medical University of South Carolina, Charleston, SC, USA.

2. Pharmacoresistant Epilepsy and VNS Therapy. September 24, 2003 presentation by J.W. Wheless, MD. The University of Texas Health Science Center, Houston TX, USA.

3. Form 10-Q for Cyberonics Inc, September 4, 2003.

4. Vagus Nerve Stimulation Therapy Mechanisms of Action. September 24, 2003 presentation by M.S. George, MD. Medical University of South Carolina, Charleston, SC, USA.

5. Form 10-Q for Cyberonics Inc, September 4, 2003.

6.Ibid.

7.Ibid.

8. Vagus Nerve Stimulation Therapy Mechanisms of Action. September 24, 2003 presentation by M.S. George, MD. Medical University of South Carolina, Charleston, SC, USA.

9. The Investigation of Vagus Nerve Stimulation Therapy in Treatment-Resistant Depression. September 24, 2003 presentation by R.L. Rudolph, MD. Cyberonics, Inc.

6.   Vagus Nerve Stimulation Therapy Mechanisms of Action. September 24, 2003 presentation by M.S. George, MD. Medical University of South Carolina, Charleston, SC, USA.

appendix c

THE IMPLANT PROCEDURE

The information on the implant procedure may sound intricate and might unfairly cloud the procedure as a dangerous operation. As you read this information, realize that medical device chest implants have been done since 1958 and the operation has been safely performed on more than 30,000 epilepsy patients.

Note: You need to rely upon the experts (neurosurgeons) to assess the risk of implanting the VNS Therapy System.

The VNS Therapy System™ consists of the VNS Therapy Pulse Generator, the Bipolar Lead, the programming wand and software, and the tunneling tool. The VNS Pulse Generator (the vagus nerve stimulator) and Bipolar Lead are surgically implanted while the patient is under general, regional, or local anesthesia. The VNS Pulse Generator is surgically implanted in a subcutaneous pocket in the upper left chest. The Bipolar Lead is connected to the VNS Pulse Generator and attached to the vagus nerve in the lower left side of the patient's neck. The patient is generally admitted to the hospital the day of surgery and discharged the same or the following day.

How does the VNS therapy work?

The VNS Therapy System™ delivers vagus nerve stimulation therapy on a continual intermittent basis. The initial standard stimulation parameters that are recommended by Cyberonics, are a thirty-second period of stimulation, which they refer to as ON time, followed by a five-minute period without stimulation, which is referred to as OFF time. To optimize patient treatment, the pulse width, output current, signal frequency, stimulation duration, and stimulation OFF intervals of the VNS Pulse Generator can be non-invasively programmed and adjusted by the treating physician with a personal computer using Cyberonics' programming wand and software. In addition, the patient can use a small, hand-held magnet that is provided with the VNS Pulse Generator to manually activate or deactivate stimulation. The magnet can also be used to provide patient control of stimulation side effects by allowing the patient to temporarily deactivate the Pulse Generator.

No one knows exactly why stimulation to the vagus nerve works. But in the various clinical trials, continuous stimulation to the vagus nerve has been shown to favorably modulate those areas of the brain that are responsible for regulating mood and depression.

The VNS Pulse Generator

The Pulse Generator of the VNS Therapy System™ is an implantable, programmable, cardiac pacemaker-like signal generator designed to be coupled with the bipolar lead to deliver electrical signals to the vagus nerve. The VNS Pulse Generator (vagus nerve stimulator) employs a battery that has an expected life of approximately eight to ten years at standard stimulation parameters. Upon expiration of the battery, the VNS Pulse Generator is removed and a new generator is implanted in a short, outpatient procedure using local anesthesia. Replacement of the lead is a different procedure. It is rarely done and is not required for routine replacement of the Pulse Generator.

Stimulator Statistics

The actual Model 102 NCP Pulse Generator is about the size of a pocket watch. It weighs less than an ounce. Cyberonics plans to introduce the Model 103 NCP Pulse Generator in 2005. The newer model will be smaller than the one currently available, the Model 102. Here are some of the statistics for the Model 102:

Weight: 8/10 of an ounce
Diameter: 2.0 inches
Thinness: ¼ of an inch thin

Model 102 Pulse Generator.

Battery Life: 6-11 years (Battery life is dependent on the
stimulation parameters determined by your
physician.)

Bipolar Lead

Cyberonics has licensed a proprietary nerve lead to convey the
electrical signal from the VNS Pulse Generator to the vagus nerve.
The lead incorporates patented electrodes that are self-sizing and
flexible, minimizing mechanical trauma to the nerve and allowing
body fluid interchange within the nerve structure. The lead's electrode and anchor tether wrap around the vagus nerve and the
connector end is tunneled subcutaneously to the chest where it is
attached to the VNS Pulse Generator. The lead for the VNS
Therapy is available in two sizes of inner spiral diameter to ensure
optimal electrode placement on different sized nerves.

Location of the implant.

Programming wand and software

The VNS Therapy System™ includes a proprietary programming wand and software, used to interrogate the device and to transmit programming information from a personal computer to the VNS Pulse Generator via electromagnetic signals. These products are compatible with both Pentium and non-Pentium-based platform personal computers. Programming capabilities include modification of the VNS Pulse Generator's programmable parameters (pulse width, output current, signal frequency, and stimulation duration and interval) and storage and retrieval of telemetry data. The VNS Therapy programming wand can be connected to a standard personal computer using a serial connector.

There are many variables that can influence the outcome of VNS therapy and they are different for each patient:

- ON/OFF Cycle: The time interval between periods of stimulation.
- Pulse Width: The duration of a single pulse within a period of stimulation. This is measured in microseconds.
- Stimulation Frequency: The number of single pulses of stimulation delivered per second, expressed in hertz.

Tunneling tool

The tunneling tool is a single-use sterile, disposable surgical tool designed to be used during surgical placement of the Bipolar Lead. This VNS Therapy tool is used for subcutaneous tunneling of the lead assembly between the nerve site in the neck and the VNS Pulse Generator site in the chest.

Notes

Source: SEC Form 10-K, Cyberonics,Inc.—July 2003.

O

appendix d

SHOULD YOU CONSIDER VNS?

Let me borrow a quote from Dr. Phil: "If you have been going to the same problem solver for ten years and you ain't gettin' any better, then you need to find a new problem solver." Change "problem solver" to antidepressants and add a Texas twang to the quote, and this may steer you to try an alternative treatment. Maybe it's vagus nerve stimulation, maybe not. But, if you are living your life with chronic depression, then something has to change.

Because the VNS Therapy System™ is not something you can purchase at your local drugstore, you will receive plenty of advice and guidance from your doctors regarding the implant procedure and your post-operation activities. For me, once I was 100 percent comfortable that the procedure was safe, there was nothing else to think about. My analysis was like the Nike commercial: "Just Do It". My family's scrutiny consisted of: "When the hell are you going to do it?!"

In life, we don't get to choose the diseases we suffer from, nor do we get to choose the potential remedy for the disease. For chronic, treatment-resistant depression, VNS Therapy is the main-stream treatment for patients who are experiencing a major depressive episode and have not adequately responded to traditional antidepressants. Rather than be intimidated by the procedure, applaud yourself for considering the most aggressive, leading-edge treatment for the biological disease of depression.

Now that I have the implant, I think there are times when my family would like to have my stimulation settings turned down!

Unlike the closely guarded secret of my shock treatments, I was much more open with friends and relatives about the vagus nerve stimulation procedure to help my depression. There is a terrible stigma associated with electroconvulsive therapy. In contrast, I didn't feel shame or embarrassment about vagus nerve stimulation. The VNS Therapy System™ is a more conventional, physical remedy to a mental health disease. Shock treatments will never be considered conventional.

With depression, sometimes the goal of treatment is to make a *very* depressed patient *less* depressed. If you have been suffering from chronic depression for a long time, a twenty or thirty percent improvement in mood can make a significant difference in the quality of your life. If I asked the 4.5 million people who suffer from the disabling disease of chronic depression, if they would take a 30 percent improvement in the quality of their day-to-day lives, I am confident every one of them would say yes.

As with any medical procedure, the common-sense advice is to temper your expectations for the outcome. It should be clear to you by now that VNS Therapy works slowly and gradually. This is not an operation where the surgeon comes out of the operating room and tells your family, "We got it (the disease) all out." It can take months for the benefits to kick in. Some patients continue to derive benefit from the pre-set continuous stimulation of the vagus nerve for up to two years after the implant. Likewise, it can take over a year before it is finally determined that VNS Therapy is not helping your depression. There is still so much to be learned about the power of this therapy and the stimulation settings that produce the optimal response in each patient.

Your decision comes down to a risk/benefit analysis. VNS Therapy is safe. That's not my opinion, it's documented by Cyberonics' epilepsy patient registry. VNS Therapy is not a cure for depression. However, in the clinical trials in which VNS Therapy was used as an adjunctive long-term treatment for chronic depression, a statistically significant number of patients achieved an Extraordinary, Highly Meaningful or Meaningful clinical benefit after twelve months of VNS.[1]

Benefits of Vagus Nerve Stimulation (VNS)

- VNS is more effective than antidepressants
- No cognitive impairment (i.e., no memory loss)
- VNS does not have the side effects of antidepressants
- VNS does not require you to remember to take your medications. Once the device is activated, there's no further action required. Compliance is guaranteed.
- Efficacy improves over time (No "Prozac™ poop out")
- Quality-of-life benefits improve over time
- No drug interactions
- VNS is not related to brain surgery

After the implant, life goes on. You continue to stick strictly to the treatment plan prescribed by your doctor. Take all of your prescribed medications; continue with psychotherapy and or a support group, take good care of yourself, and only do things you feel comfortable doing.

Both the success and failure of VNS Therapy bring their own set of challenges for the patient. You need to have your team in place to help guide you through this process. My psychologist and psychiatrist were invaluable in monitoring my progress (or lack thereof) and made adjustments as necessary.

Notes

1. Cyberonics presentation to FDA Advisory Panel—June 15, 2004.

appendix e

COMPARING ECT AND VNS

Although vagus nerve stimulation may sound simi-
lar to electroconvulsive treatments (ECT), the two therapies are
entirely different. ECT is the most effective therapy currently available for severe depression. However, because of fewer side effects
and the substantially longer sustained response, VNS Therapy™
will become the mainstream treatment for long-term treatment of
chronic depression.

History of electroconvulsive therapy

There is a stigma associated with electroconvulsive therapy
because early treatments used large electrical currents that caused
strong muscular contractions, which sometimes caused injury
(broken bones or dislocated joints). Moreover, the patients were
awake during the procedure—a terrifying experience. Everyone
remembers the dramatic (but no longer accurate) scenes in *One
Flew Over the Cuckoo's Nest*. Over the years the process has been
modified to maximize the benefit and minimize the side effects.
The amount of electricity has been decreased, patients are asleep

during the process, and muscle relaxants prevent muscle convulsions.

When is electroconvulsive therapy used?

Doctors prescribe ECT mainly to treat depression that does not respond to antidepressant medications and/or psychotherapy. While ECT is used in some cases to treat mania, schizophrenia, and catatonia, it is most useful in the treatment of depression. ECT can be the first choice of treatment for patients with psychotic depression (depression accompanied by hallucinations or delusions) and suicidal patients since it seems to start relieving symptoms after the first treatment, thereby reducing the risk of suicide.[1]

While the causes of depression are not known, abnormal chemical levels in the brain are believed to be involved. Electroconvulsive therapy is a shock treatment that induces a grand mal seizure in the brain. These seizures are similar to epileptic convulsions, where basically the brain's electrical pathways all fire at the same time. The seizure alters many chemical aspects of the brain during and after the seizure activity.

For ECT to be effective a series of treatments are required and a seizure must occur with each treatment. The patient typically receives electroconvulsive therapy three times a week for two to four weeks (at which time the depression should be gone). After several treatments, changes build up in the brain that relieve the depression. However, the changes in the brain are generally not permanent; CT scans and MRI scans taken before and after ECT show no structural changes in patient's brains. [2]

What happens during ECT?

Before an ECT treatment, patients receive a drug to put them to sleep and a muscle relaxant to prevent them from thrashing (and possibly hurting themselves) during the treatment. Patients feel nothing during ECT treatments since they are asleep.

Electrodes are placed on the head to deliver the electricity to the brain. Other electrodes on the body monitor the heart. The brain can be stimulated on one or both sides of the head, and the stimulation lasts for four seconds or less. The electricity induces the brain seizure, which lasts from 30 to 120 seconds. After the seizure ends, patients are allowed to wake up in a recovery room, and later go home until the next treatment.

What are the side effects of electroconvulsive therapy?

Side effects during electroconvulsive therapy include increased blood pressure and pulse, as well as irregular heartbeat. As with any procedure that requires anesthesia, there is a small risk of death (about 1 in 100,000). If the patient aspirates (breathes in) saliva or vomit they could develop pneumonia. In about 1 in 2,000 treatments the patient has spontaneous seizures after the end of the treatment.

When the patient wakes up after ECT, they may feel groggy, confused, nauseous, and have a headache and muscle aches. ECT also results in short-term memory loss and an impaired ability to retain new information (for example, they can't remember a new phone number). For most patients the problems with their memory usually ends a few weeks after the treatments end. However, in some cases long-term memory loss can occur.

How effective is electroconvulsive therapy?

ECT effectively ends episodes of depression in about 80 percent of patients who finish a course of ECT. However, since the brain changes that occur with electroconvulsive therapy are not permanent, there is a strong chance of the depression returning. In fact, with no further treatment, 90 percent of patients relapse in one year. Therefore, patients need further treatments, whether it is antidepressants, psychotherapy, or maintenance ECT (weekly or monthly ECT treatments).[3]

Is ECT the only choice for patients who do not respond to medication?

While ECT has been the last line of treatment for depressed patients who did not respond to antidepressant medications or psychotherapy, it does not work for all patients. In 1997, the FDA approved the vagus nerve stimulator for the treatment of epileptic seizures, and it has proved safe and effective for more than 30,000 patients. Research indicates it can also relieve treatment-resistant depression. If approved by the FDA, the Vagus Nerve Stimulator would clearly replace ECT as the treatment of choice for depressed patients.

Both ECT and the vagus nerve simulator use electrical stimulation of the brain to effect changes, but the mechanisms they use are very different. In electroconvulsive therapy, electrical stimulation of the brain causes a massive discharge of the nervous pathways in the brain, resulting in a grand mal seizure (similar to an epileptic seizure), temporarily altering the chemical makeup of the brain. The VNS Therapy Systems'™ pulse generator stimulates the vagus nerve, which in turn stimulates specific cells in the brain that favorably affect mood and depression. The pacemaker-like generator is preset to deliver stimulation to the vagus nerve on a continuous intermittent basis.

Although scientists do not know exactly how vagus nerve stimulation works, they do know that the continuous delivery of stimulation to the vagus nerve causes changes in key areas of the brain that affect depression.

One of the major problems with ECT is memory loss. The major side effect of vagus nerve stimulation is hoarseness, which is mild and tends to disappear over time. ECT therapy requires multiple treatments in a hospital setting; Vagus nerve stimulation requires one hospital visit to implant the stimulator. While ECT has been used for decades to treat depression, it is a cumbersome technique that has a strong negative stigma attached to it. The significant side effects and high relapse rate associated with ECT make it less than ideal.

Notes

1. *Electroconvulsive therapy: Treatment for depression.* Mayo Foundation for Medical Education and Research (MFMER)

2. Barklage, N. and Jefferson, J.W. *Electroconvulsive Therapy - A Guide.* 2002. Madison Institute of Medicine, Inc., Madison, WI 53717

3. *Electroconvulsive therapy: Treatment for depression.* Mayo Foundation for Medical Education and Research (MFMER)

appendix f

NEUROLOGICAL DEVICES PANEL MEETING

UNITED STATES OF AMERICA
FOOD AND DRUG ADMINISTRATION
+ + + + +
NEUROLOGICAL DEVICES PANEL of the
MEDICAL DEVICES ADVISORY COMMITTEE
+ + + + +
Seventeenth Meeting
TUESDAY, JUNE 15, 2004

The Panel met at 8:00 a.m. at the Holiday Inn Gaithersburg, Walker/Whetstone Rooms, Two Montgomery Village Avenue, Gaithersburg, Maryland, Dr. Kyra J. Becker, Chairperson, presiding.

PANEL MEMBERS PRESENT:
KYRA J. BECKER, M.D., Chairperson, University of
    Washington School of Medicine, Seattle, WA
ANDREW K. BALO, Industry Representative, DexCom, Inc.
    San Diego, California

JONAS H. ELLENBERG, Ph.D., Voting Member, Westat,
Rockville, Maryland
LAURA J. FOCHTMANN, M.D. Deputized Voting Member,
State University of New York, Stony Brook, NY
ANNAPURNI JAYAM-TROUTH, M.D., Voting Member,
Howard University College of Medicine, Washington, DC
RICHARD P. MALONE, M.D., Deputized Voting Member,
MCP Hanneman University, Philadelphia, PA
IRENE E. ORTIZ, M.D., Deputized Voting Member,
University of New Mexico, Albuquerque, NM
MARY LEE JENSEN, M.D., Director of Interventional
Neuroradiology, University of Virginia
PHILIP S. WANG, M.D., MPH, Dr.PH, Deputized Voting
Member, Brigham and Women's Hospital, Boston,MA
CRISSY E. WELLS, R.T., MBA, MHSA, Consumer
Representative, University of Virginia Health Sciences Center,
Charlottesville, VA

ALSO PRESENT:
CELIA WITTEN, Ph.D., M.D., Food and Drug
Administration, Division Director, General Restorative and
Neurological Devices

SPONSOR PRESENTERS:
RICHARD L. RUDOLPH, M.D., Vice President, Clinical
and Medical Affairs and Chief Medical Officer, Cyberonics
A. JOHN RUSH, M.D., Principal Investigator, University of
Dallas Southwestern MC, Dallas, TX
ALAN TOTAH, Vice President, Regulatory Affairs,
Cyberonics

FDA PRESENTERS:
CHANG LAO, Ph.D., Statistical Reviewer
CARLOS PENA, Ph.D., Neuroscientist, VNS Studies, Efficacy
Reviewer
MICHAEL SCHLOSSER, M.D., Neurosurgeon, Safety
Reviewer

PUBLIC SPEAKERS:
MARNA DAVENTORT, patient in the study
CHARLES DONOVAN, patient in the study
COLLEEN KELLY, patient in the study
LYDIA LEWIS, President, Depression and Bipolar Support
    Alliance
KARMEN McGUFFEE, patient in the study
IRVIN J. MUSZYNSKI, J.D., Director of the Office of Health
    Care Systems & Financing, American Psychiatric Association
LAURI SANDOVAL, patient in the study

INDEX

Charles E. Donovan, III

May 10, 2004

Janet L. Scudiero
Center for Devices and Radiological Health (HFZ-410)
Food and Drug Administration
9200 Corporate Blvd.
Rockville, MD 20850

Re: Neurological Medical Devices Panel-June 15th, 2004

Dear Doctors,
I am a patient in the D-02 study and I am writing to urge you to do everything possible in your power to unconditionally approve the vagus nerve stimulator as a treatment for chronic depression. It not just saved my life (which I didn't really care about), it changed my life.

In the spring of 1980, I graduated from Georgetown University, ironically less than 30 minutes from where the Panel Meeting will take place. I also had my first major depressive episode that same spring. I had accepted a job in the Management Training Program of what is now JP Morgan Chase and moved to New York City after graduation.

I "bounced back" during that summer. But the depression was always there lurking in the background, and depressive episodes over time became more frequent.

To keep this letter short, let's fast forward 15 years. In November of 1995, I eventually ended up in the lock-up unit of a hospital. I have very little memory of the details surrounding this hospitalization. I can only assume that my family must have had the hell scared out of them and didn't know what to do.

In 1998, I was a 39 year-old man sobbing uncontrollably, hugging my parents in the doctor's office after the psychiatrist recommended shock treatments. I had a series of 15 or so. The ECT treatments did not work, nor did any of the countless antidepressants that I tried.

In late 1999, I was no longer able to work. I don't know how I was able to continue to work as long as I did. I put up a long hard fight. It was a big mistake. The physical toll and mental toll that it took on my body was agonizing and I am still recovering physically.

In 2001, I was implanted with the vagus nerve stimulator. In my final depression rating interview (just prior to implant) with Raymond Tait, Ph.D. of St. Louis University, I simply told him that I hoped that I would die on the operating table. Given the simplicity of the procedure, it was an irrational thing to hope for, but dying would have been the "ultimate escape".

I have no idea when the device was activated or how and when it was ramped up. As recently as just a few months ago, the study investigators told me that I may never know.

All I can say is that now my life is full of genuine happiness and joy. I don't have to fake it anymore. I have lost 30 pounds in the past 18 months. I exercise regularly; swimming, Pilates and running. I am not ashamed to go to a shopping mall or other public place for fear of being noticed. Last Saturday night I attended a small dinner party, that 18 months ago, I never would have gone to. I also am working on several different projects. This is the most productive that I have been in many years.

The improvement in mood occurred very gradually over many months. But, every morning I wake up and still ask myself the same question "Is it (the depression) back?" By the time I get in the shower, the answer is the same "NO". Because the mood improvement was gradual, there was no dramatic epiphany. At this point I would have to say that the most remarkable thing is the "staying power" of the therapy. It's like the Energizer Battery, it keeps going and going.

With the information learned from the studies and the benefit of stimulation "strategy" that new patients would have (that I did not have), many desperate patients could be helped.

Unless you have personally suffered from chronic depression, you cannot truly understand it. But it's brutal.

Again, I encourage you to approve this relatively straight forward procedure, for an extremely gruesome disease. Please give the option of vagus nerve stimulation therapy to those suffering patients who are still searching for an answer, just as I had searched. Some desperate patients stop searching-forever.

Respectfully,

Charles E. Donovan, III

Brief Summary From the
Neurological Devices Panel Meeting

June 15, 2004

The Neurological Devices Panel (the Panel) met on Tuesday, June 15, 2004 in Gaithersburg, MD to discuss and make a recommendation to the Food and Drug Administration (FDA) on the approvability of the Cyberonics, Inc. PMA, P970003/S50 for the Vagus Nerve Stimulator (VNS) Therapy System intended for the adjunctive long-term treatment of chronic or recurrent depression for patients over the age of 18 who are experiencing a major depressive episode that has not had an adequate response to two or more antidepressant treatments. The Panel membership for this meeting consisted of four psychiatrists, one interventional neuroradiologist, two neurologists, a statistician, a consumer representative, and an industry representative.

The sponsor presented its information on the safety and effectiveness of the device, and FDA reviewers summarized the data in the PMA. After deliberations on the information in the submission, the Panel considered FDA's questions.

The Panel then voted five to two to recommend that FDA approve the PMA with conditions. The recommended conditions of approval are as follows:

1.   Patients should have failed four or more trials of traditional treatment modalities for treatment-resistant depression (medications and electroconvulsive therapy) prior to use of the device.

2.   The device be implanted by surgeons with appropriate training.

3.   Training regarding device electronic programming be provided for primary care providers.

4.   Additional patient labeling for use of the device and identification card be provided.

5.   A patient registry to collect clinical data be established.

6.   The physician labeling be revised regarding the following: 12 month open label follow-up, the variable effect of treatment, patient selection, and deletion of imaging claims.

The Panel members who voted against conditional approval believed a new study was necessary to establish a reasonable assurance of safety and effectiveness of the device.

Contact: Janet L. Scudiero, Executive Secretary, at 301-594-1184 ext. 176 or jls@cdrh.fda.gov.

Transcripts of this meeting may be purchased from:
Neal R. Gross and Company
1323 Rhode Island Ave., N.W.
Washington, D.C. 20005
202-234-4433 or 800-473-1433 and

Food and Drug Administration
Freedom of Information Staff (HFI-35)
5600 Fishers Lane, Rockville, MD 20857 301-443-1726 (fax)

O

appendix g

INSURANCE ISSUES

"One of the benefits of participating in the investi-gational clinical trial for VNS Therapy was that I couldn't beat the price of the implant procedure: it was FREE. There was no fighting with an insurance company for pre-approvals; no in-network, out-of-network, or reimbursement issues; or having a bill kicked back unpaid after the treatment.

You, unfortunately, will not have that advantage. The good news, though, is I believe ultimately the majority of insurance companies will cover a large percentage, if not 100 percent, of the cost of VNS Therapy. Depending on where you live and other factors, the cost of the implant procedure, follow-up, changing the device settings, stimulation levels, etc., is around $25,000.

According to Cyberonics, 99.9 percent of all insurance companies cover the identical procedure for pharmaco-resistant epilepsy patients. Effective January 1, 2004, Medicare actually raised the level it reimburses hospitals for the VNS Therapy System™ by 23.7 percent, to just over $24,000. This information is posted on the CMS (Centers for Medicare and Medicaid Services) Web Site: http://www.cms.hhs.gov and published in the Federal Register. In an environment where Medicare was slashing reimbursement rates across the board, this increase was a clear endorsement of the value of the VNS Therapy System™.

Because of Cyberonics' experience in epilepsy and negotiating reimbursement issues with insurance companies, a lot of the groundwork has been done for reimbursement for the depression indication. All of the major insurance companies are now familiar with the procedure. The only change is the diagnosis (chronic depression). I have listed below the insurance codes for the vagus nerve stimulator implant:

- The Stimulator: A4649

- The two incisions: 61885, 64573

- Intra-operative programming of VNS Therapy System: 95970, 05974, 95975

As we all know, insurance companies blatantly discriminate against mental health patients. I have tried to do my part by writing Congress to urge my support for passage of the Wellstone Mental Health Parity Act (see Appendix I). Unfortunately, Congress once again failed to reach an agreement on the passage of this critical piece of legislation in 2004.

It is impossible to predict exactly how insurance companies will reimburse VNS for depression. Insurance companies are giant bureaucracies, with multiple layers of people whose only job is to say no. Each insurance company is different; each policy is different. This potential challenge calls for reinforcements and you may need all the ammunition you can get. So, I have enlisted the help of the Patient Advocate Foundation. The Patient Advocate Foundation is a national non-profit organization that seeks "equal access to health care for all Americans." They are a superb, caring organization that truly puts the patient first.

You may have to play an active role in getting your treatment approved and the Patient Advocate Foundation has provided a step-by step plan of action. On the following pages, I have reprinted a portion of the Foundation's *Your Guide to the Appeal Process*.

Your Guide To The Appeal Process
VOLUME II

Patient Advocate Foundation
700 Thimble Shoals Boulevard
Suite 200
Newport News, VA 23606
Tel: 757. 873.6668 1. 800.532.5274 Fax: 757.873.8999
Email: info@patientadvocate.org
Internet: http://www.patientadvocate.org/

COPYRIGHT © 2000 by PATIENT ADVOCATE FOUNDATION

MISSION STATEMENT
Patient Advocate Foundation is a national non-profit organization that serves as an active liaison between the patient and their insurer, employer and/or creditors to resolve insurance, job discrimination, and/or debt crisis matters relative to their diagnosis through case managers and attorneys. Patient Advocate Foundation seeks to safeguard patients through effective mediation assuring access to care, maintenance of employment and preservation of their financial stability.

ACKNOWLEDGMENTS
Your Guide to the Appeal Process was inspired by patients and family members who work diligently at fighting a disease and for the right to treatment. The Patient Advocate Foundation would like to thank the doctors, nurses, and other professionals who assist patients and their families in these battles everyday. We would especially like to thank patients and professionals who were willing to discuss their needs and concerns which brought about the idea for this brochure.

Patient Advocate Foundation would like to gratefully acknowledge the generous support of Amgen, Inc. in underwriting the research of the first edition of *Your Guide to the Appeal Process* through an unrestricted educational grant.

We thank Janet Patton, RN, BSN, a Patient Advocate Foundation employee, for her writing of this book. We express our gratitude to the following members of our Editorial Review Board:

John D. Blum, Associate Dean for Health Law Programs Loyola University, Chicago Illinois Professor of Law

Marc DeBofsky, Esq., DeBofsky & DeBofsky, Chicago, Illinois

Howard B. Hellen, Esq. San Diego, California

Marc Lippman, MD, Georgetown University Medical Center, Washington, DC

Richard P. Neuworth, Esq., Lebau & Neuworth, LLC, Baltimore, Maryland

The Patient Advocate Foundation would like to thank the Editorial Review Board for their thoughtful review, insightful comments, and expert advice.

Your Guide To The Appeal Process

INTRODUCTION

Dealing with an injury or illness is stressful for the patient as well as the family. When you or a loved one are denied a medical procedure or therapy that has been performed or requested to be performed by your treating physician, it can precipitate a crisis situation. Since each insurance policy is different, it would be impossible to write a fail proof plan that would work for each patient in all situations. Each patient and each situation is unique. This brochure is designed to help patients and their loved ones navigate the appeal process. It contains suggestions and advice. It should not be interpreted as a substitute for legal counsel.

It is also important to point out that support from your treating physician and specialist is critical. Your physician is the professional trained to assess and recommend a treatment plan for you.

Simply stated, a "denial" means that the insurance company has decided not to pay for the procedure or therapy that your doctor has recommended. The procedure or therapy may have already been performed or may be scheduled in the near future. If the denied procedure has not yet been performed, the insurer may be denying the request for pre-authorization. "Pre-authorization" means that the insurer has given approval for a member to receive a treatment, test, or surgical procedure before it has actually occurred. The goal of the appeal process is to allow the patient to be heard and provide any and all necessary information to convince the insurance company to change their decision and provide coverage for the procedure. This brochure is also designed to provide a logical approach to the appeal process. When submitting your appeal, keep in mind that the best defense is a good offense. In other words, it is generally better to take the time to gather all the necessary information and submit a well thought out appeal packet than to hastily submit a response and miss the opportunity to educate the insurance company about your specific situation. There are several steps you should take to produce a thorough appeal packet. These steps are:

1. gather preliminary information
2. understand the illness and the insurance
3. write the appeal letters
4. evaluate the result

Step 1: Gather Preliminary Information

If you do not already have a file and a notebook to document all correspondence, start one now. You should keep a record of all letters you receive and a log of all telephone calls you make or receive related to the denial. Over time you may forget people's names and dates. This documentation will help you stay organized and focused on your goal. There are specific questions you need to ask once you are notified the procedure will not be covered through pre-authorization.

- When did you receive notice of the denial?
- How did you receive notification of the denial?
- Did your doctor notify you directly, or did the administrator or insurer notify you directly?

- Did you receive a letter or phone call from the insurance company?
- Did you receive a statement from your insurance company stating that your bills will not be paid?

First and foremost, **you need to get a copy of the denial letter.** Under the Employee Retirement and Income Security Act (ERISA), your denial letter should include a **specific reason** for the denial and a reference to your plan explaining the basis for the denial. For example, is your insurance company denying paying for your treatment because it considers it to be experimental? Or, do you belong to an HMO that does not have out-of-network benefits and you wish to go to an out-of-network provider? Place a call to the doctor's office and find out what information was submitted to the insurance company and ask for a copy of the information and the letter written by your doctor requesting payment authorization. If your requests are ignored, you should put them in writing to make a record of your attempts to obtain the information you need.

If you have received a denial for a procedure that has already taken place and there are bills that are unpaid, you need to begin to backtrack to find out why.

- Does your insurance company require procedures to be pre-authorized?
- If so, did your doctor's office pre-authorize the procedure?

This brings up the most important documents you have and need: your plan document and plan summary, or health insurance booklets. The plan document and plan summary are essentially a contract between you and the insurance company. You need to be sure that you have a current copy. If you do not have a copy, you must write to the plan administrator and request that a copy be sent to you. Under ERISA, these documents must be sent to you within thirty days of the written request or the company may be assessed penalties. **READ** your plan language. What does it say about your procedure and specific reason for denial? Under ERISA, a specific reason for denial must be stated in language that would be understandable to an employee. If the procedure was to be pre-authorized, do you or does your doctor have a copy of the authorization or the approval from the insurance company? If no pre-authorization was required review specific exclusions listed in your plan. If your treatment is not identified as a specific exclusion, you need to begin your appeal.

- Who can you contact to discuss the denial?

Step 2: Understand the Illness and The Insurance

You need specific names and numbers of contact people. The denial letter from the insurance company may contain this information. You may need to call the insurance company and ask for a contact person. Be sure to ask for that person's direct line. Ask the staff at your doctor's office who you can call to ask questions and get any letters or records you may need. If you will be receiving your treatment at a facility away from home, be sure to have the name and number of your treating doctor's nurse. You will likely need to get letters from the treating doctor as well. You also need to be sure that you have a written copy of the steps that you must take in order to appeal the denial. This information should be in your plan document. It may also be in the denial letter. You may need to request this information from the insurance company. Be sure you understand each step of the appeal process. It is your path to obtaining reimbursement.

By answering these questions and collecting these documents you have the initial information you need. You have your plan document, your denial letter and you have the names of the contact people at the insurance company and the doctor's office. Now you must begin to educate yourself and continue to research the issue to achieve your goal of reimbursement. If you still do not understand your rights or the appeal process is unclear, and the employer or insurer will not or cannot explain further, it may be helpful to contact an attorney. (See "When to Consult an Attorney")

You need to understand your condition or your loved one's condition before you can discuss the case with the insurance company. It is very important that you understand exactly what the doctor wants to do and why it is necessary. Read any copies of the letters your doctor may have submitted to the insurance company. The initial letter typically discusses the patient's case in simple medical terms and then explains what the doctor proposes to do. This letter is often referred to as the "treatment plan" or "plan of care". You can also ask your doctor or nurse to explain it further. Often they may have written material that may be helpful, or they may be able to direct you in finding more information.

You need to be familiar with the type of insurance you have. If your insurance is through your employer or your spouse's employer, call the benefits manager and ask him or her to explain the coverage. For example, is the employer self-insured and does the employer contract with a third party to administer the plan? Or does the employer contract with an outside company to administer the plan **and** pay the claims? It makes a difference because you may be able to get your denial overturned by working with the benefits manager or the designated representative of Human Resources. If the company is not self-insured, explaining the problem to the benefits manager, both verbally and in writing, may be very beneficial. The benefits manager can, in some situations, put enough pressure on the insurance company to get the denial overturned. Also, if the employer has had problems with the insurer they may choose not to renew the contract with that insurance company.

Step 3: Write the Appeal Letters

After you have gathered the preliminary information and have a basic understanding of the illness and the insurance policy, you are ready to start the appeal process. Some appeals are handled by the doctor's office or the clinic or the hospital. In this situation, the patient is usually put in contact with a case manager who has experience in the appeals process. In this case, the patient should understand the steps in the process and should "oversee" what is being done. It is suggested that the patient request copies of all letters and correspondence to and from the insurer. The patient should also be in close contact with the case manager or person handling the appeal for them.

In other situations, the patient and family are informed of the denial and they must handle the appeal on their own. If this is the case, you must manage your appeal. Your appeal should include:

- An appeal letter.
- A letter from your doctor and specialist addressing specifics of your case.

- Any pertinent information from your medical records.
- Any articles from peer-reviewed clinical journals that support your case that illustrate medical efficacy.

Your Appeal Letter

The purpose of the appeal letter is to tell the insurance company that you disagree with their decision and why you believe they should cover the procedure. The letter should be factual and written in a firm but pleasant tone. When writing your appeal letter you should include:

- *Your identification.* This includes your policy number, group number, claim number, or other information used to identify your case.
- The reason for the denial that they explained in the denial letter.
- A brief history of the illness and necessary treatment. Typically this information will be included in the doctor's letter in detail but it can also be helpful to add a shorter and less complicated version in the patient's letter.
- The correct information. If you believe the decision was made because of an error, state the correct information, i.e. is the denied procedure different from the requested procedure? Maybe a coding error was made and the insurance company believes you will be receiving a different drug.
- Why you believe the decision was wrong. Specific information based on facts to show that the treatment should be provided, i.e. you may have to go out-of-network for a procedure but only because the procedure is medically necessary according to your doctor and there is no in-network provider for the treatment.
- What you are asking the insurance company to do. Typically you are asking that the insurer reconsider the denial and approve coverage for the procedure in a timely manner.

Sample Appeal Letters

The Sample Appeal Letters included in this guide are designed to be a general guide for your specific letter. Sample Appeal Letter A was written as though the denial was based on a question of medical necessity. Sample Appeal Letter B addresses the issue of a denial based on "out of network" benefits. Each patient and each denial are unique. It is recommended that you read each letter and then identify other important details that need to be added to your letter. You must also remain factual. It is very important that your denial letter be focused on the intended outcome.

Your Doctor's Appeal Letter

You should also ask your doctor and your specialist to write a letter discussing your specific case and why your treatment is medically necessary. The letter should be addressed to the person at the insurance company that sent you the denial letter, or directly to the medical director at the insurance company.

It should include:

- Any information about your illness that your doctor feels is clinically important.
- The prescribed treatment plan.
- Why the treatment is medically necessary.

Medical Records

Ask your doctor and specialist if there are any documents in your medical records that may be helpful in your appeal. For example, it may be helpful to send a pathology result documenting the specific cell type. In the case of certain cancers, the insurance company may need to see what chemotherapy drugs you have already received. In some cases the insurance company may ask to see specific documents from your medical records.

Articles from peer-reviewed clinical journals

Often an insurance company will deny a procedure because they believe there is not enough evidence that the procedure is helpful for a specific disease. If you and your doctor believe this is the basis for your denial, you need to submit documentation that

Sample Letter A

[Date]

[Name]
[Insurance Company Name] [Address]
[City, State ZIP]
Re: [Patient's Name] [Type of Coverage]
[Group number / Policy Number]

Dear [Name of contact person at insurance company],

Please accept this letter as [patient's name] appeal to [insurance company name]'s decision to deny coverage for [state the name of the specific procedure denied]. It is my understanding based on your letter of denial dated [insert date] that this procedure has been denied because:

[Quote the specific reason for the denial stated in the denial letter.]

As you know, [patient's name] was diagnosed with [disease] on [date]. Currently Dr. [name] believes that [patient's name] will significantly benefit from [state procedure name]. Please see the enclosed letter from Dr. [name] that discusses [patient's name]'s medical history in more detail.

[Patient's name] believes that you did not have all the necessary information at the time of your initial review. [Patient's name] has also included with this letter, a letter from Dr. [name] from [name of treating facility]. Dr. [name] is a specialist in [name of specialty]. [His/Her] letter discusses the procedure in more detail. Also included are medical records, and several journal articles explaining the procedure and the results.

Based on this information, [patient's name] is asking that you reconsider your previous decision and allow coverage for the procedure Dr. [name] outlines in [his/her] letter. The treatment is scheduled to begin on [date]. Should you require additional information, please do not hesitate to contact [patient's name] at [phone number]. [Patient's name] will look forward to hearing from you in the near future.

Sincerely,

Sample Letter B

[Date]

[Name]
[Insurance Company Name] [Address]
[City, State ZIP]
Re: [Patient's Name] [Type of Coverage]
[Group number / Policy Number]

Dear [Name of contact person at insurance company],

Please accept this letter as my appeal to [insurance company name]'s decision to deny coverage for [state the name of the specific procedure denied]. It is my understanding based on your letter of denial dated [insert date] that this procedure has been denied because:

[Quote the specific reason for the denial stated in the denial letter.]

I have been a member of your [state name of PPO, HMO, etc.] since [date]. During that time I have participated within the network of physicians listed by the plan. However, my primary care physician, Dr. [name] believes that the best care for me at this time would be [state procedure name]. At this time there is not a physician within the network who has extensive knowledge of this procedure. Dr. [name of primary care physician], a plan provider, has recommended that I have the procedure done outside the network by Dr. [name of specialist] at [name of treatment facility].

I have enclosed a letter from Dr. [name of primary care physician] explaining why he recommends [name of procedure]. I have also enclosed a letter from Dr. [name of specialist] explaining the procedure in detail, his qualifications and experience, and several articles that discuss the procedure.

Based on this information, I am asking that you reconsider your previous decision and allow me to go out-of-network to Dr. [name] for [name of specific procedure]. The procedure is scheduled to begin on [date]. Should you require additional information, please do not hesitate to contact me at [phone number]. I look forward to hearing from you in the near future.

Sincerely,

the procedure is effective. This documentation should be in the form of articles that come from the professional journals or "magazines" that doctors use to keep up to date on the latest treatments. These journals have editorial boards of physicians who specialize in specific areas of medicine. That is what makes a journal "peer reviewed". This type of documentation has become very popular with the insurance companies and it is very common for them to request this type of documentation. Your physician and specialist have probably had such a request for information in the past and they can assist you in obtaining these articles.

These four pieces of information should be put together in a "packet" and be submitted to the insurance company by registered mail or some other form that you will be able to track and find out who signed for the information. This will alleviate the excuse that the information was "never received". You should keep a duplicate copy of all the information you are submitting and add it to your file. You may wish to call to confirm receipt of your materials.

After the denial has been received and your appeal has been submitted, the next thing to do is wait for a response. Waiting can be the hardest part. Your plan probably gives a length of time that the insurance company has to respond to your appeal. If it does not, you need to ask the benefits manager or the insurance company when you will be notified of the response. If you are unable to get a response, you may want to consider legal counsel. (see "When to Consult an Attorney")

Sample Appeal Letters

The Physician 's Sample Appeal Letter is also a general guide for a specific letter. Most physicians have written appeal letters many times. Some are far removed from the appeal process and are unsure of the specifics of your denial. They may also be unsure of the amount of information necessary. It is important that you communicate the specific reason for the denial to your treating physician and ask that they write their appeal letter with enough information to address the denial specifically.

Physician's Sample Appeal Letter

[Date]

[Name]
[Insurance Company Name] [Address]
[City, State ZIP]

Re: [Patient's Name] [Type of Coverage]

[Group number / Policy Number]

Dear [Name of contact person at insurance company],

It is my understanding that [Patient's name] has received a denial for [name of procedure] because it is believed that the procedure is [state specific reason for the denial i.e. not medically necessary, experimental, etc.].

As you know, [patient's name] has been under my care since [date] for the treatment of [state disease]. [Give a brief medical history emphasizing the most recent events that directly influence your decision to recommend the denied therapy.]

For this reason I am writing to provide you with information regarding [name of procedure]. [Give a brief, yet specific description of the procedure and why you believe it should be approved.]

I have also included several journal articles supporting the use of [name of procedure] for [patient's name] [name of disease].

I ask that you reconsider your previous decision based on the information above. I believe therapy should begin on [date]. Should you have any questions, please do not hesitate to call me at [phone number].

Sincerely,

Step 4: Evaluate The Result

If you receive a phone call or a letter informing you that your denial has been overturned and the insurance company will cover the procedure, CONGRATULATIONS! Before you celebrate you need to request a copy of the approval letter. You also need to be sure that you are aware of any conditions that are included. For example, you may get an approval to have the surgical procedure, but the insurance company may only cover it if it is performed by one of the doctors in their plan that you have never seen. If the conditions are unreasonable and unacceptable to you, discuss them with your doctor and insurance contact person. You may consider continuing with the appeal process. Most plans have several levels of appeal.

If your appeal has been denied, you also need a copy of the second denial letter. Like your original denial letter, this letter must also contain the specific reason for denial. Read the letter carefully. It may have a different reason for the denial. For example, the original denial letter states that a bone marrow transplant was denied because it was not effective for the disease, and was to be performed "out-of network". You submitted your appeal and all the appropriate documentation. The second denial letter rejects the procedure because "there was not enough evidence provided to show that the transplant is medically necessary". These are very different reasons for denying the same procedure.

Typically, the second level of appeal will be reviewed by a different group of people at the insurance company. Usually your second denial letter will explain the reason for denial and may even ask that you submit specific information that was not received with your first appeal letter. Be sure to notify your doctor of the decision and the new information that is needed. This denial letter may instruct that if you are interested in appealing further that you send your letter and new information to a different person. If you decide to continue with the appeal process, you should submit another appeal packet with new information specifically addressing the current reason for denial. Again, keep copies of all information and send the packet registered mail, return receipt requested. If your appeal is again denied, you should request the third denial in writing and notify your doctor. If you believe your insurance company should cover the procedure and are willing to proceed with the appeal process, you should refer to your plan document for the next step.

At this point some insurance companies will offer you what they call an "external review". This means that the insurance company will send your appeal to a company that they contract with who will review the denial, the appeal, and any new information and make a recommendation to the insurance company about the procedure in question. The external review board is typically made up of nurses, attorneys, and doctors who specialize in the specific procedure you are asking the insurance company to cover. In some states the law allows the patient to request that your case be sent for an external review. To date, the following states have external review boards:

Arizona	California	Connecticut
Florida	Hawaii	Illinois
Maryland	Minnesota	Missouri
New Jersey	New Mexico	New York
Ohio	Pennsylvania	Rhode Island
Tennessee	Texas	Vermont

If you live in a state who has an external review board, you can contact the state department of insurance for further information.

While external review can be very beneficial, it is important that the limitations are clear. The external review company can only act within specific parameters. They cannot override your policy. They can make decisions based on your policy guidelines. For example, you need to have surgery and want an "out-of-network" doctor miles from your town to perform the surgery but you have a policy with no out-of-network benefits. Your insurance company agrees that you need the surgery and has an in-network surgeon in your town. If the surgeon in your town is in-network and is qualified to perform the surgery the external review board would probably not be helpful because of the nature of your request. However, if you and your surgeon believe that the surgeon in your town is not qualified to perform the surgery for a specific reason and you can support this with the necessary documentation, the external review board may be able to substantiate your claim. That may result in the insurance company overturning your denial.

At this point, if you have exhausted all the levels of appeal and are not satisfied with the decision, your remaining alternative may be to pursue the issue in court.

When to Consult an Attorney

This is an important question and one that is asked frequently. There is no right or wrong answer. Many people feel more secure discussing their case with an attorney when they receive the denial. Others would rather appeal the decision on their own to see if they can overturn it without legal help and expense. For some it depends on the cost of the procedure that has been denied. It may make more sense to seek legal advice if the procedure costs $100,000 than if the procedure costs $1000. As previously mentioned, if you do not understand the appeal process or you are unable to get answers from your employer or insurance company, an attorney may be helpful to advise you of your rights and options. This is an individual decision. If you decide to seek legal advice you should consider the following:

- Select an attorney with experience in healthcare law.
- Discuss the legal fees up front and request a detailed billing.
- Determine at what point the attorney will take over the case.

Some patients will completely exhaust the administrative appeal process before they ask an attorney to take over the case. It is imperative that you make every effort to have an attorney involved in the case throughout the administrative appeal process in the event you wish to pursue the case later in court.

Others to Notify

Insurance and patient's rights are a hotly debated political issue. Patients often ask if it is helpful to notify their state and local representatives of their insurance issues. In some cases it has been helpful. Other times, patients get nothing more in return than a form letter stating there is nothing their legislator can do. You may choose to approach this question by asking yourself, "What do I have to lose?" You are already preparing your own appeal letter. You could easily send a copy of your denial letter and your appeal letter to your legislators asking for any assistance they can provide. You may access a list of legislators by state at the PAF website: http://www.npaf.org.

It may also be beneficial to notify your State Department of Insurance. The duties of the insurance commissioner and the Department of Insurance vary from state to state. One of the main objectives is to be sure the insurance company is following the patient's policy. The Department of Insurance may also be aware of any state laws that may come in to play in a specific case. Many states require that problems be reported by the patient in writing and may even require that their forms be filled out. It can be helpful to notify the Department of Insurance in your state when you receive the original denial. You can call them to request a copy of the necessary paperwork to submit your complaint.

In some rare instances it may be necessary to contact the media. This is recommended only if you have tried at length to resolve the problem and have enlisted the help of your legislators and the Department of Insurance with no resolution.

Expedited Review

If you have received a denial for a procedure that must be performed within a specific time frame, you and your doctor need to communicate that to the insurance company immediately. Most states have laws protecting patients in an emergency. That may be different if the procedure must be started in near future. Most insurance companies already have a plan in place for such occurrences and their guidelines will be different. If you do not feel that you are making progress toward your goal and time is short, you may choose to consult an attorney to advise you of your rights and options.

When to Contact the Patient Advocate Foundation

You may contact the PAF at any point in the process for our advice, guidance, and support. The appeals process is very complicated. It requires you to gather information and write letters. You need to keep a notebook and a file for documentation. You need to remain courteous and polite when working with your insurance company, while you are dealing with the stress of an illness. You now know what steps to take to appeal your denial. Take this process one step at a time.

Take it one day at a time. The PAF would be happy to answer any questions you may have. To reach the Patient Advocate Foundation:

753 Thimble Shoals Blvd., Suite B
Newport News, Virginia 23606
Tel: 1.800.532.5274 -or- 757.873.6668
FAX: 757.873.8999
E-mail: help@patientadvocate.org
Internet: www.patientadvocate.org

References

Aetna will allow members to appeal denials. (1999) Associated Press. http: //www. insure. com/health/zzaetnareview 199.html

Decarlo, T. (April, 1999) The top ten HMO mistakes, how to avoid them. New Woman, pp. 86-119.

Frey, H. (1998). How to protect yourself in the age of managed care. http://www.patientadvocacy.net/pac4.htm

Greene, Jan. (1998) Some HMOs now let you appeal. http://www.onhealth.com/ch1/columnist/item,34478.asp

Help for health insurance customers. (1999) National Association of Insurance Commissioners.
http://www.insure.com/health/naic-kit998.html

Never talk to the monkey when the organ grinder is available. (January, 1998). http://www.integsoft.com/appeals/tal/monkey.htm

Practical Tips for the Practicing Oncologist. (1997) American Society of Clinical Oncology. Chapter 18, pp. 83-84.

Reimer, S. (1995). What to do when denied health or disability benefits. (Spring, 1995) The CFIDS Chronicle, p. 37.

Taking control of your health care. A guide to getting the most from your health plan. Pamphlet by: Citizens for the "Right to Know".

Timely solutions for improving oncology provider case manager communications. (1998). Independent Study module by Oncology Education Services.

You have a VOB, now make 'em pay. (January, 1998) http://www.integsoft.com/appeals/tal/vob.htm

appendix h

Psychology Today Magazine's 101 Facts About Depression

The following information is reprinted with permission from *Psychology Today's Blues Buster: The Newsletter About Depression*, May 2004. Here is the latest information about the disease as presented at the 2004 Annual Meeting of the *American Psychiatric Association*:

Depression is not in your head. It's in your brain. It is now seen as a neurodegenerative disorder, associated with long-term brain injury. Prolonged depression may result in progressive and cumulative damage to the brain.

The longer you stay depressed, the greater the chances you will not come out of it. Something about depression is toxic.

Depression is best characterized as a syndrome of cellular dysfunction in stress-modulating/mood-regulating brain cells.

Approximately 35 percent of depression is the result of genetic vulnerability. Fully 65 percent of the risk comes from life events. Stress leaves its mark on the brain.

Anxiety increases the risk of subsequent depression fourfold. Eighty-five percent of those with depression have an anxiety disorder first.

Anxiety disorders begin early, in childhood, and affect twice as many girls as boys.

More than 10% of people have some anxiety disorder in any 12-month period, and surveys of freshman college students over the past 40 years indicate that anxiety levels of young people are increasing.

People who experience physical and sexual abuse, parental loss or neglect before puberty are most subject to mood and anxiety disorders later in life. Such events permanently alter the reactivity of the central nervous system, leading to an outsize response to stress.

Those whose depression is linked to adverse events early in life respond better to psychotherapy than to antidepressant drugs.

Experts now see depression as the result of maladaptive interactions between the emotional centers of the brain and the higher "executive" areas, which are responsible for maintaining control in response to stress.

One gene implicated in a depression is the transporter gene for serotonin. A specific variation of the gene seems to predispose people to anxiety-related personality traits, aggression and hyper-excitability of emotional regions of the brain in response to emotionally significant stimuli.

Persons with major depression and panic symptoms have a lower rate of response to treatment than other persons, it takes longer for them to respond, and they are most likely to experience residual symptoms despite treatment.

Depression feeds itself. If you have one depressive episode you have a fifty percent chance of another. If you have two depressive episodes you have a seventy percent chance of another.

Major depressive disorder is more common among white Americans (10.4%) than among African Americans (7.5%) or

Mexican-Americans (8%). But low-grade depression, or dysthymic disorder, is more common among blacks (7.5%) and Mexican-Americans (7.4%) than among whites (5.7%)

Between 1990 and 2001, the number of children diagnosed with depression increased 2.4-fold, from 12.9 per 1,000 children and adolescents to 31.1. The percent of patients prescribed an antidepressant increased from 44.4% to 59.3%. In 1990, 207% of such children received an SSRI; 39.7% did in 2001.

Substance abuse is the rule, not the exception, in bipolar disorder.

Alcoholism is far more common in persons with bipolar disorder (up to sixty percent prevalence rates have been reported) than among persons with unipolar depression (16.5% or the general population (13.8%). Both alcoholism and bipolar disorder are marked by impulsivity.

Bipolar disorder is typically misdiagnosed. Some research shows that the condition is diagnosed correctly in only 20 percent of cases.

Bipolar disorder occurs with greater than normal frequency among persons with cluster headaches and those who are subject to migraine headaches.

Even during manic episodes, those who suffer from bipolar disorder have the same negative thought patterns and core beliefs about the self that are seen in persons with major depression. The findings suggest that cognitive psychotherapy may benefit bipolar patient as well as persons with major depression.

Children of a parent with bipolar disorder are themselves at increased risk for any of a number of psychiatric disorders, from unipolar depression to substance abuse.

Depressed persons with a history of alcohol abuse appear to be at increased risk of suicide, even if they are not currently abusing alcohol.

Anger attacks in depression appear to reflect vascular disease. Brain imaging studies show a higher incidence of lesions in the white matter among those with depression who experience anger attacks.

Physical inactivity is a risk factor for major depression among adolescents. Low levels of vigorous exercise and high levels of sedentary activities constitute independent risk factors for developing depression over the next year.

Cigarette smoking is far more prevalent among those with psychiatric disorders than among the general population. In one survey, nearly fifty percent of bipolar outpatients had a history of smoking, thirty-five percent were current smokers.

One of the many neurobiological changes that occurs in depression is decreased ability to generate nerve growth, likely the toxic effect of over activity of the stress response system. The lack of nerve growth may account for the inflexibility of thought processes and memory problems that accompany depression.

Pregnancy does not protect against occurrence or relapse of mood disorders. Six percent of pregnant women suffer from major depression.

In over 50% of cases, the symptoms of postpartum depression actually begin during pregnancy.

One of two women with major depression during pregnancy will still suffer from depressive and/or anxiety disorders six months postpartum.

Maternal depression during pregnancy has significant developmental effects on infants. Infants of depressed moms have poorer orientation skills, decreased muscle tone, lower activity levels. It also has negative effects on temperament.

Given the emerging risks of new or recurrent maternal depression on infants, it is not necessary sound advice for women to discontinue medications in the event of pregnancy.

Acting as a caregiver is psychically demanding. In one study of older persons caring for a family member who had suffered a stroke, fully thirty percent developed depression.

Most persons with bipolar disorder also have at least one other psychiatric condition and take multiple psychoactive drugs.

A large-scale clinical trial of the anti-mania drug quetiapine shows that it is also effective against the depressive symptoms of bipolar disorder. The new trials suggest that quetiapine may work solo, simplifying treatment for a disorder that normally involves the use of multiple agents. The drug also improved a broad range of anxiety and mood symptoms associated with bipolar depression.

Depression is not only the most pervasive feature of bipolar disorder but it has been particularly resistant to treatment. It is also associated with suicide attempts.

From 50% to 80% people with major depression experience problems of diminished libido and arousal.

Sexual problems are also prominent side effects of antidepressant drugs. The sexual side effects of the serotonin reuptake inhibiting drugs (SSRIs) may diminish more than sexual drive and performance. They may jeopardize the impetus to fall in love, stay in love or get out of a destructive relationship.

Men are most likely to have problems with desire and orgasm. Women are more likely to have problems with arousal.

Studies show that the combination of drug therapy and psychotherapy is often most effective against depression; delivering the psychotherapy after there has been some response to medication may prove most effective.

Among the emerging ways to enhance the effectiveness of and to speed response to current antidepressant and anti-anxiety medication is the use of so-called atypical antipsychotic agents as adjuncts; these drugs are commonly used to treat bipolar disorder and schizophrenia.

Depression most often produces physical as well as psychological symptoms, and frequently presents as pain in the absence of physical illness.

Persons with major depression are four times more likely to have chronic pain than those without depression.

On average, pain precedes depression by three to five years. One way pain may lead to depression is by disrupting sleep.

The present of pain symptoms predicts poor response to standard antidepressant drug treatment.

Chronically depressed women are most likely to experience somatic symptoms of depression.

By itself, pain multiples the risk of depression approximately fourfold.

Whether pain leads to depression or depression leads to pain is not clear. There are common pathways of neurotransmitters that may explain the overlap.

Pain accompanies anxiety, too, even in the absence of depression.

Adults with attention-deficit disorder have nearly triple the risk of suffering from major depression as well. They have more than five times the risk of bipolar disorder.

Testosterone levels naturally decline in aging men, but the hormone does not seem to play a role in major depression. Decreasing hormone levels may play a role in low-grade depression known as dysthymia, involving symptoms like low libido and fatigue.

Testosterone supplements do not work as a treatment for major depression: Small doses may slightly increase sex drive. Large doses have erratic effects, making some men euphoric and some men angry and irritable.

Sex hormones are known to affect brain functioning. The risk of depression for women transitioning to menopause is higher than normal. The Harvard Study of Moods and Cycles found that women who had never before been depressed were three times more likely to become depressed during the transition; women who had intense hot flashes and other symptoms had six times the risk. Both estrogen replacement therapy and standard antidepressants helped improve mood in menopausal women.

The same study also found that women with heavy menstrual flow or irregular periods are more likely to suffer from depression.

Depression and insomnia are closely linked: More than three-quarters of people with bipolar disorder have insomnia, and sleep difficulties are the single best predictor of episodes of mania in people with this form of depression.

Medical illness is a risk factor for major depressive disorder. While antidepressants are effective, they are less so in people with both depression and physical illness.

The most common reason for discontinuation of antidepressant medication is side effects. Such complaints as gastrointestinal disturbance, agitation and headache often begin with initiation of treatment.

Sexual dysfunction, sleep disturbance, weight gain and cognitive blunting may begin early in treatment and persist after remission.

Sex hormones such as estrogen and progesterone are known to modulate brain function. The abrupt changes in estrogen and progesterone may underlie development of mood disturbances around menopause.

Unipolar major depression is the second leading cause of medical disability in the United States for women, just after heart disease. For men, it is the tenth leading cause of medical disability.

The evidence is stacking up that dramatic changes in the American diet in the past 100 years affect nutritional elements that are critical to nervous system function and thus may play a significant role in major mental health problems. These include fatty acids, B vitamins, antioxidants and chromium. Nutrients are chemicals that affect genes and can switch them on and off.

Depression is associated with shrinkage of the brain, most notably in the hippocampus, a region crucial to memory and other cognitive functions. The effects may be reversible-if depression is treated in time

In addition, another region of the brain, the amygdala, often referred to as the fear center, grows larger.

The brain changes seen in major depression have also been found in persons with bipolar disorder: decreased size of the hippocampus, and increase in the amygdala. The more symptoms of depression patients experience, the greater the brain changes.

All antidepressant drugs work by turning on nerve growth in the brain. Neurogenesis is essential for modulation of feelings.

Exercise also stimulates the growth of new neurons, which may explain why studies show it is an effective treatment for even moderate to severe depression.

The weight gain associated with anti-depressant drugs may represent the body's attempt to elevate blood sugar and force glucose into the brain as a way to fuel the high metabolic demands of neurogenesis.

Psychotherapy and antidepressant drugs both produce measurable-but different-effects on the brain.

Psychotherapy works against depression from the top down, providing cognitive tools that patients can use to interrupt and redirect emotionally relevant stimuli coming through the fear center and other parts of the brain.

The drugs most commonly used against depressions, the SSRIs, may not be effective against pain symptoms even if they alleviate depression.

Evidence suggest that antidepressants that act on levels of norepinephrine as well as on serotonin-so-called dual-reuptake inhibitors-may be more effective in treating depression accompanied by physical symptoms such as pain.

At least thirty percent of patients with depression do not respond to a first course of treatment with SSRI antidepressants.

Only about thirty-five to forty percent of patients achieve full remission after a 6- to 8-week course of antidepressant drug treatment, but increasingly full remission is recognized as necessary for full return to function as well as prevention of relapse.

A new double-blind study shows that the omega-3 fatty acid DHA (docosahexaenoic acid) may be an effective treatment for depression. However, more is not always better. DHA appears to work best at the dose of 1 gram a day. Higher amounts may result in an "overcorrection effect" on fatty acid balance.

Symptoms such as fatigue and sleep problems are most likely to persist after treatment with antidepressant drugs. Some studies show that addition of the drug modafinil may be helpful; a stimulant used to combat sleepiness and improve alertness, it also enhances mood and memory.

The stimulant modafinil may be most useful as adjunctive therapy in persons with so-called atypical depression. Despite the name, atypical depression is an especially common form of the disorder, marked by fatigue, sleepiness and carbohydrate craving often leading to significant weight gain.

Women with bipolar disorder who are treated with anti-seizure medications may be at increased risk for development of osteoporosis.

Patients receiving SSRIs who remain on drug therapy for more than 90 days incur lower annual medical costs than patients who discontinue medication.

appendix i

HAMILTON RATING SCALE FOR DEPRESSION

The Hamilton Rating Scale for Depression (HRSD) instrument is designed to be used only on patients already diagnosed as suffering from affective disorder of the depressive type. It is used for quantifying the results of an interview and its value depends entirely on the skill of the interviewer in eliciting the necessary information. The scale contains seventeen variables measured on either a five-point or a three-point rating scale, the latter being used where quantification of the variable is either difficult or impossible. Among the variables are: depressed mood, suicide, work and loss of interest, retardation, agitation, gastrointestinal symptoms, general somatic symptoms, hypochondriasis, loss of insight, and loss of weight.

Scoring the Hamilton Depression Rating Scale (HDRS)

The total HDRS score provides an indication of the level of a patient's depression and, over time, provides a valuable guide to a patient's progress. In general, the higher the total score, the more severe is the depression. While it is not realistic to categorically assign a specific level of depression to a specific HDRS score, it is possible to give the following general guidelines:

HDRS Score:	Level of depression:
10 - 13	Mild
13 - 17	Mild to Moderate
> 17	Moderate to severe

The seventeen questions are designed to be administered by a healthcare professional and are used to rate the severity of depression in patients already diagnosed as depressed.

Hamilton Rating Scale for Depression

This questionnaire cannot replace an evaluation by a professional, but it can familiarize you with the symptoms of depression and give you an idea if you may meet the diagnostic criteria for clinical depression.

Appropriate for: Patients diagnosed with depression

Administered by: Physician or trained raters

Time to complete: 30 minutes

Summary: HRSD/HAM-D is a 17-item observer-rated scale to assess the presence and severity of depressive states where anxiety-related symptoms are prevalent and no other depressive symptoms are present.

9 items are scored 0-4, whereas the further 8 are scored 0-2, as these represent variables that do not lend themselves to quantitative rating (0=absent; 1=doubtful or slight; 2=mild; 3=moderate; 4=severe. 0=absent; 1=doubtful or slight; 2=clearly present).

A score of 10 is generally regarded as indicative of a diagnosis of depression.

Conducted in semi-structured interview carried out by trained a clinician.

Benefits of HRSD
- Widely used: HRSD and HAM-D are the most widely used instruments for clinical assessment of depressive symptoms.
- Well-validated: The tool was developed in 1960 and since that time has been widely evaluated and established as a highly reliable and valid assessment tool.
- 'Gold'-standard of depression rating scales.
- Frequently used in studies as an anchor with which to compare newer instruments.

To rate the severity of depression in patients who are already diagnosed as depressed, clinicians administer this questionnaire. The higher the score, the more severe the depression.

For each item, write the correct number on the line next to the item. (Only one response per item)

1. DEPRESSED MOOD (Sadness, hopeless, helpless, worthless)
   - 0= Absent
   - 1= These feeling states indicated only on questioning
   - 2= These feeling states spontaneously reported verbally
   - 3= Communicates feeling states non-verbally-i.e., through facial expression, posture, voice, and tendency to weep
   - 4= Patient reports VIRTUALLY ONLY these feeling states in his spontaneous verbal and nonverbal communication

2. FEELINGS OF GUILT
   - 0= Absent
   - 1= Self-reproach, feels he has let people down
   - 2= Ideas of guilt or rumination over past errors or sinful deeds
   - 3= Present illness is a punishment. Delusions of guilt
   - 4= Hears accusatory or denunciatory voices and/or experiences threatening visual hallucinations

3. SUICIDE
　　0= Absent
　　1= Feels life is not worth living
　　2= Wishes he were dead or any thoughts of possible death to
　　　　self
　　3= Suicidal ideas or gesture
　　4= Attempts at suicide (any serious attempt rates 4)

4. INSOMNIA EARLY
　　0= No difficulty falling asleep
　　1= Complains of occasional difficulty falling asleep-i.e., more
　　　　than 1/2 hour
　　2= Complains of nightly difficulty falling asleep

5. INSOMNIA MIDDLE
　　0= No difficulty
　　1= Patient complains of being restless and disturbed during
　　　　the night
　　2= Waking during the night-any getting out of bed rates 2
　　　　(except for purposes of voiding)

7. INSOMNIA LATE
　　0= No difficulty
　　1= Waking in early hours of the morning but goes back to
　　　　sleep 2= Unable to fall asleep again if he gets out of bed

8. WORK AND ACTIVITIES
　　0= No difficulty
　　1= Thoughts and feelings of incapacity, fatigue or weakness
　　　　related to activities; work or hobbies
　　2= Loss of interest in activity; hobbies or work-either directly
　　　　reported by patient, or indirect in listlessness, indecision
　　　　and vacillation (feels he has to push self to work or activi-
　　　　ties)
　　3= Decrease in actual time spent in activities or decrease in
　　　　productivity
　　4= Stopped working because of present illness

9. RETARDATION: PSYCHOMOTOR (Slowness of thought and speech; impaired ability to concentrate; decreased motor activity)

    0= Normal speech and thought
    1= Slight retardation at interview
    2= Obvious retardation at interview
    3= Interview difficult
    4= Complete stupor

10. AGITATION

    0= None
    1= Fidgetiness
    2= Playing with hands, hair, etc.
    3= Moving about, can't sit still
    4= Hand wringing, nail biting, hair-pulling, biting of lips

11. ANXIETY (PSYCHOLOGICAL)

    0= No difficulty
    1= Subjective tension and irritability
    2= Worrying about minor matters
    3= Apprehensive attitude apparent in face or speech 4= Fears expressed without questioning

11. ANXIETY SOMATIC: Physiological concomitants of anxiety, (i.e., effects of autonomic overactivity, "butterflies," indigestion, stomach cramps, belching, diarrhea, palpitations, hyperventilation, paresthesia, sweating, flushing, tremor, headache, urinary frequency). Avoid asking about possible medication side effects (i.e., dry mouth, constipation)

    0= Absent
    1= Mild
    2= Moderate
    3= Severe
    4= Incapacitating

12. SOMATIC SYMPTOMS (GASTROINTESTINAL)

0= None

1= Loss of appetite but eating without encouragement from others. Food intake about normal

2= Difficulty eating without urging from others. Marked reduction of appetite and food intake

13. SOMATIC SYMPTOMS GENERAL

0= None

1= Heaviness in limbs, back or head. Backaches, headache, muscle aches. Loss of energy and fatigability

2= Any clear-cut symptom rates 2

14. GENITAL SYMPTOMS (Symptoms such as: loss of libido; impaired sexual performance; menstrual disturbances)

0= Absent 1= Mild 2= Severe

15. HYPOCHONDRIASIS

0= Not present

1= Self-absorption (bodily)

2= Preoccupation with health

3= Frequent complaints, requests for help, etc. 4= Hypochondriacal delusions

16. LOSS OF WEIGHT

A. When rating by history:

0= No weight loss

1= Probably weight loss associated with present illness 2= Definite (according to patient) weight loss

3= Not assessed

17. INSIGHT

0= Acknowledges being depressed and ill

1= Acknowledges illness but attributes cause to bad food, climate, overwork, virus, need for rest, etc.

2= Denies being ill at all

Total Score

Source: *Journal of Neurology, Neurosurgery and Psychiatry*, 1960: v 23, p 56-61.

appendix j

HISTORY OF VNS AND DEPRESSION

FDA GRANTS EXPEDITED REVIEW STATUS TO CYBERONICS'S NCP SYSTEM for the Treatment of Depression

HOUSTON, July 26, 1999 /PRNewswire/ — Cyberonics, Inc. (Nasdaq: CYBX) today reported that the United States Food and Drug Administration (FDA) granted Expedited Review status for a future Premarket Approval Application for the Cyberonics' NCP System for the treatment of major depressive episodes in patients with unipolar and bipolar depressive disorder. FDA grants Expedited Review status in order to provide for more effective treatment or diagnosis of life-threatening or irreversibly debilitating diseases or conditions. FDA grants Expedited Review status to devices which are intended to treat or diagnose such diseases and conditions, and which typically represent a breakthrough technology which may provide major (not incremental) increased effectiveness or reduced risk compared to existing, FDA-Approved therapies.

According to recent World Health Organization (www.who.int/inf-fs/en/fact217.html) and other studies, depression is a major public health problem in the United States and worldwide. Depression was the number one cause of disability worldwide in 1990, with 340 million people suffering from major depression. The incident of depressive illness increases with age, and depression is expected to be the second leading cause of disease burden in 2020. In the United States, an estimated 6 million people are being actively treated for depression. Recurrence (multiple episodes) of depression runs as high as 80% of cases. An estimated 1 million people in the United States suffer from treatment resistant chronic depression. An estimated 1 million people worldwide and 100,000 people in the U.S. are treated annually with electroconvulsive therapy (ECT). Depression is a very expensive and life-threatening disorder. Depression costs in the United States are estimated at $40 billion a year in lost work and health-care costs, $12.4 billion of which are direct treatment costs. A depressed person is 35 times more likely to commit suicide and 15% of chronic depression cases end in suicide.

# #

Cyberonics, Inc. Announces Start of Pivotal Clinical Study of Vagus Nerve Stimulation in Depression

U.S. Food and Drug Administration Approves Final Study Protocol; First Five Clinical Sites Are Initiated with Patient Enrollment Now Underway

HOUSTON, Aug. 2, 2000 /PRNewswire/ — Cyberonics, Inc. (Nasdaq: CYBX) today announced the start of the pivotal clinical study of Vagus Nerve Stimulation (VNS) with the Cyberonics NeuroCybernetic Prosthesis System (NCP(R)) for the treatment of depression. The U.S. Food and Drug Administration (FDA) has approved the final study treatment protocol (D-02) and the first five clinical study sites have been initiated by Cyberonics. The University of Minnesota is the first D-02 Study site to enroll a patient.

Additionally, the University of Miami, Saint Louis University, Medical University of South Carolina in Charleston, and Baylor College of Medicine in Houston have also been initiated and have begun enrolling patients with nine total patients now enrolled. Cyberonics anticipates that the study will include a total of 210 implanted patients at 20 sites. The remaining sites are expected to be initiated by December of 2000, and enrollment in the clinical study is projected to conclude in the summer of 2002. The approved protocol for the D-02 Study calls for a randomized, double-blind, placebo-controlled study with similar inclusion and exclusion criteria used in the depression pilot clinical study. As D-02 study sites are initiated, they will be listed on the Cyberonics web site at www.cyberonics. com/depression. Patients interested in the study may also contact Cyberonics at 888-748-1652 to obtain information about the location of the study sites."

# #

Cyberonics Announces Final Implant in 21-Site, Phase III U.S. Pivotal Study of Vagus Nerve Stimulation for Depression

HOUSTON--(BUSINESS WIRE)--July 11, 2001--NeuroCybernetic Prosthesis System Implanted in 235 Patients,

Preliminary Study Results Likely Available by March 2002

Cyberonics, Inc. (Nasdaq:CYBX) today announced that the 235th and final patient received and implant of the NeuroCybernetic Prosthesis (NCP(R)) System as part of the company's expanded U.S. phase III pivotal study of vagus nerve stimulation (VNS) for chronic or recurrent depression. In June 2001, Cyberonics received approval from the United States Food and Drug Administration (FDA) to expand the original study protocol from 210 to up to 240 patients.

Robert P. ("Skip") Cummins, Cyberonics' chairman and chief executive officer, commented, "The FDA approved Cyberonics' request to expand the depression pivotal study in two weeks, and within three weeks of that approval, the final implant occurred. The additional patient experience will strengthen the study and should not result in any delays. The last pivotal study patient should complete the acute phase of the study by the end of October and we remain on track to release the preliminary results of the depression pivotal study by March 2002."

VNS therapy is delivered by the Cyberonics NCP System, an implantable medical device similar to a cardiac pacemaker, which delivers mild electrical stimulation to the left vagus nerve in the patient's neck. Implantation of the stimulation generator and electrode is typically done on an outpatient basis in approximately one hour. Various mechanism of action studies suggest that VNS modulates activity in the areas of the brain responsible for mood, motivation, sleep, appetite and alertness.

# #

appendix k

MENTAL HEALTH ADVOCACY

Charles E. Donovan, III

September 30, 2003

The Honorable William Clay
House of Representatives
Washington, DC 20515

Dear Representative Clay,

I am writing to urge Congress to take up and pass now the Senator Paul Wellstone Mental Health Equitable Treatment Act, legislation to end blatant and widespread discrimination against people with mental illness.

Mental illness is the second leading cause of disability and premature mortality in the United States. Yet every day families with "good health coverage" discover that their loved ones who have mental illnesses cannot get needed care because their insurance sets strict limits on mental health treatment - like ending further coverage after a limited number of treatment sessions - but imposes no such limits on treating any other illness.

These practices are not only unfair, they're irrational. Mental illnesses are reliably diagnosed and for virtually every mental disorder, there is a range of treatments and services that have been shown to be effective.

Health insurers who erect these barriers to medically necessary mental health treatment inflict enormous harm on American families...and on our economy. These discriminatory practices - which are applied only to mental disorders - cause illnesses to go untreated and worsen. Tragically, this lack of care leads all too often to unemployment, broken homes, school failure, and even suicide. Untreated mental illness also costs our economy about $80 billion each year -- in lost productivity, sick leave, and unemployment.

American families need a solution NOW. The solution is bipartisan legislation that would require simple parity between mental health benefits and the benefits provided to treat any other illness or injury. This simple, fair step will save lives and families.

As studies have shown, mental health parity legislation will not lead to a significant increase in insurance premiums or in the number of uninsured Americans. But the costs of NOT enacting parity are high, and will fall most heavily on taxpayer-funded public programs, our economy, and the well-being of American families and their communities.

Please make passage of a strong mental health parity bill a top priority before Congress adjourns this year.

Sincerely,

Charles E. Donovan,III

Charles E. Donovan, III

Via Fax

January 19, 2004

The Honorable Bill Frist,M.D.
Dirksen Senate Office Building
Washington, D.C. 20510

Re: The World Health Care Congress-January 25th-27th, 2004

Dear Senator Frist,

I read in today's Wall Street Journal, that you are listed as one of the speakers scheduled to give a "Visionary Address" at this ground break- ing U.S. Leadership Forum to Transform Health Care Costs and Quality.

I would like to urge you to speak out against the blatant and wide- spread discrimination against people with mental illness. Health insurers, including Medicare, discriminate reimbursement levels against mental illnesses versus any other type of illness.

Untreated mental illness costs the economy $80 billion a year and unquantifiable human suffering.

As you speak in front of our country's health care leaders, please make a top priority, the passage of a strong mental health parity bill by Congress.

Sincerely,

Charles E. Donovan

Charles E. Donovan, III

August 13, 2004

Secretary Tommy G. Thompson
U.S. Department of Health and Human Services
200 Independence Avenue, S.W.
Washington, D.C. 20201

Dear Mr. Secretary,

Yesterday, 4.5 million desperate Americans, suffering from the life-threatening disease of chronic depression, were deprived of the safe and effective option of vagus nerve stimulation therapy (VNS). The FDA, in an unprecedented decision, ignored the recommendation of its Medical Device Advisory Panel to approve this therapy, and considered the PMA-Supplement non-approvable.

VNS Therapy saved my life. Thirty thousand epilepsy patients have been safely implanted with VNS. In a shocking decision, FDA not only ignored the recommendation of its panel of experts, but also the strong recommendations of numerous psychiatric thought leaders and the compelling testimony and needs of people with treatment-resistant depression who today have no long-term treatment for their lifelong and life-threatening illness.

The FDA's mission as stated on its Web Site:

No regulated product is totally risk- free. FDA will allow a product to present more of a risk when its potential benefit is great—especially for products used to treat serious, life- threatening conditions."

In my opinion, 35,000 suicides committed annually and 500,000 annual suicide attempts serious enough to warrant an emergency room hospital visit, qualify for "life-threatening conditions."

Please do everything in your power to reverse this indefensible decision. 4.5 million Americans and their families are depending on you.

Respectfully,

Charles E. Donovan

About the Author

Charles Donovan is a study patient in the clinical trial for the investigation of vagus nerve stimulation as a long-term treatment for chronic depression. He was implanted with the device in April 2001.

On June 15, 2004, he was a presenter at the FDA Medical Device Advisory Panel meeting in Washington, DC, where the Panel recommended FDA approval of vagus nerve stimulation.

A graduate of Georgetown University, Donovan began his career in the management training program of what is now JPMorgan Chase.

He is the editor of the www.VagusNerveStimulator.com Web Site and Bulletin.

Currently he lives depression-free in St. Louis, Missouri.